D1287057

THE HOURS OF THE PASSION

The Hours of The Passion

By JUDE MEAD, C.P.

THE BRUCE PUBLISHING COMPANY
MILWAUKEE

NIHIL OBSTAT:
RALPH GORMAN, C.P.

IMPRIMI POTEST:
VERY REVEREND ERNEST WELCH, C.P.
Provincial

NIHIL OBSTAT:
JOHN A. SCHULIEN, S.T.D.
Censor librorum

IMPRIMATUR:
✠ ALBERT G. MEYER
Archiepiscopus Milwauchiensis
December 13, 1955

Rosary College Dewey Classification Number: 232.96

Library of Congress Catalog Card Number: 56-6947

Preface

SINCE that memorable day and fateful hour in which Jesus Christ lay down His life as the Nicene Creed attests, "for us, and for our salvation," the cross and the Passion is rightly the center of all Christian theology, liturgy, and mysticism. The sign of the cross surmounts our cathedrals and our most far-flung mission stations. We are signed with the cross and have the merits of the Passion poured out on us from birth to death in the sacraments of holy Church. In the Mass, our central sacrifice, the mystery of Calvary is re-enacted in time before our eyes. The penny catechism protests, "The sign of the cross is the sign of the Christian."

Before Mary taught men the mysteries of the Rosary, before Crusaders and monks brought back the Way of the Cross to Europe, countless generations of Christians, and great numbers of saints, prayed the Passion with the Hour Books of medieval devotion. The psalms and the prayers of the Church were set in order to remind men of the hours of the Passion. Dramatic illustrations of Passion scenes frequently accompanied these provoking thoughts painstakingly inscribed by hand.

In the early eighteenth century God raised up the last of the Crusaders and the last great monastic penitent of modern times, St. Paul of the Cross. At Mary's request he was to teach the people how to meditate on the bitter Passion of the blessed Christ and to help them to be mindful of Christ's sufferings, and grateful to the God who had endured so much for them.

PREFACE

In the pages of this little book I hope the spirit of the Hour Books of old is caught for the reader, and the mission of St. Paul of the Cross continued in a modern world. That many will be brought remembrance and gratitude to Jesus Crucified for His blessed Passion is the only purpose for this modern Book of Hours.

Thanks are due to *The Sign* magazine, Union City, N. J., where these chapters first appeared; the meditation outlines were prepared especially for this book.

JUDE MEAD, C.P.

Contents

THE HOURS OF THE PASSION

The Hour of Darkness

THE Middle Ages, the ages of Faith, produced a most practical devotion in the Book of Hours. These were prayer books with a thought for each hour of the day. They were profusely illustrated for the benefit of the many devout souls unable to read, as well as for the devotion of the learned.

From earliest times there has been a tendency to associate the scenes of the Passion of Christ with the hours of the day and night. Such a pattern gave orderliness to one's reflection. It gave ease to recollection and a change from the tedium of superficial repetition.

In the primitive Church we had the watches of the day and night, modeled after Roman military practice, which eventuated into the "hours" of the Divine Office.

Medieval Christians preferred the Passion for the meditations in their Hour Books.

In the painfully stilted atmosphere of the Counter Reformation the "Clocks of the Passion" appeared. These represented the face of a timepiece, on which a scene of Christ's Passion was stated conformably to the hour. The antique devotion was telescoped.

Even in modern times this device has been used, as for example, in Father Gallway's book *Watches of the Passion*. In these meditations, however, the idea of the Book of Hours will be followed, as a merely mechanical device.

The historical Christ, our Blessed Lord, was of course true God and true man. So spontaneously did He unite Himself with us that He chose "Son of Man" as His own preferred title. Although this title was first applied to the God-Man by Daniel (7:13), Christ used it of Himself more than seventy times in the New Testament.

Another interesting sidelight is the fact that our Redeemer not only identified Himself as a man in the world but He constantly associated Himself with, and circumscribed Himself by, time. He limited Himself frequently to the present by saying, "now." He even went further and spoke of the very hour of things. He placed Himself or things in the hour over one hundred times.

Thus when we call our Lord "The Man of the Hour," it is not totally for effectiveness. It is as it were by His own choice and preference. It is done in these meditations, because time has proved that the association of scenes from the Passion of Jesus with the hours of the day and night has always been an easy and ready means to increase and foster true devotion in the hearts of the Christian faithful.

In our present way of speaking we refer the expression "man of the hour" to one who at the moment is riding the crest of a wave of popularity, due to his daring or efficiency or appeal to the general public. But how quickly the hour of a man passes. Daring gives way to dotage, efficiency to incapacity, and the appealing diffidence of youth to the dependence of old age.

There is only One Man whose courage is forever. Only One whose effectiveness increases with the time. Only One who never ages, and whose hour is forever. And this is "the Man, Christ Jesus" (1 Tim. 2:5). His courage is a lesson for all who suffer, His daring a challenge to every man. His work on the cross so efficacious that it moves beyond earth to heaven, beyond time to eternity. His appeal as a loving Saviour, who died forsaken and alone in the flower of His youth is also an ideal after which the hearts of all are drawn. "And I, if I be lifted up, will draw all things unto myself" (Jn. 12:32).

Jesus Christ is the Man of the Hour. Every hour is His triumph.

Roughly speaking, the Passion of our Lord began after His discourse at the Last Supper, when He went out to the Garden of Gethsemani. Christ the God-Man set down once and for all the nature of this dread hour when He said to His enemies: "This is your hour, and the power of darkness" (Lk. 22:53).

It was about midnight when Jesus came with His chosen band of Apostles to the seclusion of the Garden of Olives. The paschal moon is now on high. It floods the Garden of Olives with a misty light. The trees spin lacy shadows across the rocky land. We see a group of tired men, oblivious of the beauty of the night. They are asleep. A little further on we see three more men, Peter, James, and John. Like the rest of the Apostles, they too are asleep. Alone, there is one Man who watches and prays. It is the Lord.

The silence of the night is broken by an anguished cry. "My Father! If it be possible, let this chalice pass from me. Nevertheless, not as I will, but as thou wilt" (Mt. 26:39). Then the God-Man turns to His chosen three. They are asleep. "Could you not watch one hour with me?" He asks them, and then returns to His lonely vigil.

Like an echo that would not be dissipated, again His prayer is heard: "My Father, if this chalice may not pass away, but I must drink it, thy will be done" (Mt. 26:42).

A second time He finds His disciples asleep. Only the moon, the stars, and the gnarled trees are willing to watch with the lonely Christ. "And being in an agony, He prayed the longer, and his sweat became as drops of blood, trickling down upon the ground" (Lk. 22:43).

This is the scene of Christ's agony in the garden. This Man who is prostrate with sorrow and bathed in His own blood is the Son of God. What is this awful mystery that has come to pass?

Jesus Christ is about to begin His Passion. Even now His enemies are on the way against Him. He could escape. He could summon twelve legions of angels. He could strike dead anyone who would dare to approach Him. But no. He will do nothing to save Himself. So He waits alone in the moonlight. He awaits His Passion. This is why He had come into the world. This is to be the crowning glory of His life.

But death is a hard thought for any man. And Christ is perfect man as well as perfect God. A violent death, known beforehand, makes the thought of death even harder. An undeserved death, death for crimes one has not committed, is the worst outrage a man can endure. So the innocent Christ awaits His death. His violent death. His violent and undeserved death. The spiderweb pattern of trees, silhouetted against the sky, reminds Him of the dragnet closing in about Him, ever nearer and nearer. It is the hour of darkness and of the Prince of Darkness.

Is it any wonder that our Lord is sorrowful? Is it any wonder that He collapses to the ground under the strain? Is it any wonder that He cries out to be delivered from this catastrophe? His mind, His will, and His Sacred Heart repress the dreadful fear that encompasses His body.

He sees all the wickedness of a wicked race envelop Him. He feels all the sins men commit by speech choking at His throat. He is nauseated by the picture of the sins men commit by thought. Impure thoughts, murderous thoughts, hateful thoughts. He is the all-pure God, and yet He must suffer for these vile abuses of the intellect of man. His body is tortured as it repels all the sufferings it must endure to atone for the sins which men have committed, and will commit, against their own bodies, or the bodies of others. Truly He is in an agony. There is no one to help Him. His best friends are asleep. The night wind sighs. The dry earth drinks His blood.

Then, as if the thought of sin were not enough to convulse His sacred frame, the thought comes to Him of the thousands for whom He will suffer in vain. The men and women for whom His death will be useless. Those who love sin and perish in it. The night is pierced with sobbing. Sobbing from the heart of God. With a great cry, with blood and sweat and tears, Jesus Christ is struggling alone against fear, sin, death, and hell. What a spectacle!

An angel comes to encourage Him. Slowly He rises. He looks as white as a corpse from the loss of blood. He is shaking as a reed in the wind. His agony is over. He will face death alone. He has submitted His will to the Father's, becoming obedient until death.

St. Vincent de Paul recommends blessing the hour as a sure means to recollection of spirit. When the clock strikes, his spiritual children were to be mindful of God's presence, offer Him anew the work at hand, and beg grace to carry the work to perfection.

In this first hour of the Passion of Jesus Christ, what an example we behold! This first hour is cleansed and sanctified with the Blood of Jesus. This first hour is offered unequivocally to the will of God. In this first hour is grace and fortitude poured out by the ministering angel.

For many souls, the first hour of the day is the hardest hour of their lives. To arise from sleep and to face the vexing, sometimes seemingly insuperable obstacles and problems of everyday routine. For the sick, there loom long hours of loneliness and conscious suffering. For workingmen, jobs that are hard and unloved but necessary to support their family or parents. For mothers, endless household tasks – the children, and the inroads on their patience. For those in unhappy and even unholy situations, the dread of another day to be lived with their unhappy selves.

What is the answer? Moderns tell us it's a musical alarm clock, a breakfast in bed, or a dry cereal that will explode in your face and thus brighten your first waking hour. But these are material and childish substitutes for reality for a materialistic and childish generation which dreads reality.

However, real things come easy to Christian people. If the first hour of the day is your rough hour, don't look down for help but look up. Offer the first hour to God in union with the first hour of His Passion. That hour which He dreaded beyond all else. That hour in which He tried to have His burden eased. That first lonely hour when He accepted the will of God at so great a cost to Himself that His very blood burst His veins.

Make the first hour of every day your best hour by uniting it with Christ in the Garden. Show Him that you are willing to watch with Him. Drive out sleep and despair with the strength of the Passion. Be mindful that God will not ask of you the great things He asked of His only Son. Be resigned to the will of God. In the first hour offer Him every thought, word, and action of the day and your reward will be peace.

Many things heretofore left undone will be accomplished because they are being done for God. Many useless and sinful things will be avoided, as we wouldn't dare to offer God such works as our debt to Him. Get off to a good start. Our Blessed Lord tells you – "This is your hour" (Lk. 22:53). Make the most of it. Keep the Man of Sorrows as your model. Follow in His footsteps, and make Him the Man of the Hour, for every waking hour of your life.

How to Meditate Further on This Chapter

COMPOSITION OF PLACE

a) *Physical:* Picture in your mind's eye the Garden of Gethsemani: the rocky ground, the gnarled olive trees, the silence, the moonlit enclosure, and the towers of the city of Jerusalem on the opposite hill.

b) *Spiritual:* Jesus Christ is lonely; He is neglected. There is no one to mourn with Him or to comfort Him. He begins His Passion with a prayer of resignation on His lips.

WHO IS IT THAT SUFFERS?

This is the good God who created man in a Garden of Delights. This is He who is made like to men in all things except in sin. This is He from whom virtue has gone out. Who went about doing good. This is the Lamb of God who takes away the sins of the world.

WHAT DOES HE SUFFER?

a) *Spiritually:* He suffers in His holy soul. "My soul is sorrowful unto death." He suffers from spiritual dryness.

b) *Mentally:* Jesus suffers in His holy heart. He is neglected. "Could you not watch one hour with me?" He is betrayed by one of His own. He is tormented by the devil with the ingratitude of sinners. He fears the death of the body. He is disgusted by the multitude of the sins of the human heart. He wants to be delivered, but is resigned to God's will for Him. "Not my will, but thine be done."

c) *Physically:* Christ suffers in His sacred body. His very blood bursts His veins and trickles down upon the ground. He is shaken from head to foot with agony. He is engaged in a deathlike struggle – the separation of His blood from His body.

WHY DOES HE SUFFER?

a) *Chronologically:* From the fear of death. From the ingratitude of men. From the disgust He has for sin. From loneliness. From indifference. From being let down by those He loved. From an agony of soul. From the heroicity of His act of resignation to God's holy will. From the imminence of His blessed passion.

b) *Mystically:* For my sins of thought, word, deed,

and omission. For my neglect of His grace. From my indifference to His ordeal. From my lack of prayer. From my want of resignation to the will of God in my daily life. From my recoiling from penance and sufferings.

WHAT AM I GOING TO DO ABOUT IT?

Resolutions: To make my morning offering every day. To accept hard things in a true spirit of penance for my sins. To avoid the near occasions of sin. To think frequently on the agony of Jesus in the garden, that I may never again betray Him by sin.

PRAYER

O Lord Jesus Christ, who in the garden has taught us to pray by word and by example, that we might overcome temptation: mercifully grant that we may always be devoted to prayer, and may merit to attain its abundant fruit: Who livest and reignest forever. Amen.

ASPIRATION

Sacred Heart of Jesus, strengthened in Thine agony by an angel, strengthen us in our agony (*300 days' indul.; Racc. No. 239*).

The Wakening Hour

TWO o'clock is the waking hour. According to medieval legends, the stillness of the night is broken at this hour by the rousing and stirring of animals. Incidents are cited where even the cock crowed at this hour. And the pious conclusion was that it was at this hour of the night that Jesus Christ was born into the world among the dumb beasts, who saw and comprehended according to the testimony of Isaias, "The ox knoweth his owner and the ass his master's crib" (Isa. 1:3). This, then, is the reason why the Hour Books of the Middle Ages abound in barnyard-life portraits when prayers and thoughts are suggested for the second hour of the day. Robert Louis Stevenson, in his "Travels with a Donkey," confirms this phenomenon of the waking hour for animals.

Our Blessed Lord is true man as well as true God. Every hour is His. And every hour is His triumph.

In the narrative of the Sacred Passion, the second stage was the betrayal of Jesus Christ by the traitor, Judas. It was well into the second hour of the morning that the betrayer and his henchmen invaded the Garden of Gethsemani and disturbed the stillness of the night.

This becomes in fact the waking hour. The Apostles are roused. They awake half dazed from sleep. They stand in a frightened, gesticulating, perplexed group – sheep soon to be dispersed, their Shepherd struck.

Our Blessed Lord needs no awakening. He stands almost detached from the things that are going on. He knows that He has been betrayed for a sum of money. And money was the last thing in the world to interest Jesus Christ.

Even a casual reading of the life of Christ as related in the four Gospels impresses the reader with Christ's contempt for money. When St. Peter was accosted by the tax collector, Christ paid the tax for both Peter and Himself with a coin taken from the mouth of a fish. The sight of the money-changers in the temple brought on the righteous indignation of Christ, who drove them away with a whip.

Christ was Lord of heaven and earth and had no need of money. He warned the Apostles about the dangers of carrying a purse. Only one of the Apostles was allowed to carry what little money the Twelve possessed. We are but little surprised, then, to read that when Judas sold Christ, the price was cheap – almost insignificant – the price of a slave.

Christ cared not for money. But what Judas lost was priceless. What Christ wanted most, Judas took from Him. Christ wanted love, and loyalty, and the salvation of souls. When Christ was betrayed, His love was wasted. When Christ was betrayed, His loyalty was cast aside. When Christ was betrayed, an apostle became an apostate and despaired of salvation. The betrayal cost Christ dearly, not in money, but in heartbreak and disappointment; and this, because of the ingratitude of one of His own.

BRAMANTI

Alone and unaided, our Lord had suffered an agony of soul so great that He had sweat blood. In the distance He now sees His enemies approaching. "Arise, let us go hence," He tells the drowsy Apostles. He that is to betray me is at hand" (Mt. 26:46). The armed band draws nearer. Angry faces lower in the torchlight. The Apostles are alarmed. They are somewhat reassured when they see Judas. After all, he is one of their own. But Christ is not deceived. He knows why Judas is here. The heart of Christ is sick when He beholds Judas the hypocrite.

Christ loved Judas. He trusted him. Christ thought enough of Judas to have him as a chosen companion. He made Judas an Apostle and ordained him a priest at the Last Supper. For three long years Christ had taught him by word and example. They were intimate friends. Our Lord let Judas see Him work miracles, gave Judas this same wonderful power. Christ had also trusted Judas because He had named him treasurer of the apostolic band. What numberless gifts in both the natural order and the supernatural order, Christ had given Judas. Little wonder the heart of Christ was broken at the sight of Judas.

This was a moment of disappointment because Christ tried so hard to save Judas. He had declared openly, "You cannot serve two masters" (Mt. 6:24). He had condemned those who loved money; those who were covetous; those who let the desire of money bring them to ruin. Still Judas had not heeded. When gentle teaching had failed, Christ sounded a warning. He let all know that He knew someone was plotting against His life. "Have I not chosen you twelve, and one of you is a devil" (Jn. 6:71). At the Last Supper, Christ solemnly declared: "One of you is about to betray me!" (Mk. 14:18.) When all the disciples asked, "Is it I, Lord?" Judas hid his guilt under the same question. Our loving Saviour did not betray the traitor publicly.

But even this great charity of Christ had no effect on Judas. When he arose to leave on his errand of violence, Christ called after him a last reminder that his perfidy was known: "That which thou dost, do quickly" (Jn. 13:27). Then St. John tells us that Judas went out . . . "and it was night" (13:30). There is something about that remark of St. John that is sinister and foreboding. The scene of the betrayal in the Garden of Olives is the climax of the dark deed in the Passion of Christ.

Christ stands with His Apostles as they await the band approaching them. The Apostles are not quite sure what all this is about but Christ knows. His Sacred Heart is heavy over the treachery of this chosen Apostle. How little response has been given to the pleas and warnings of Christ! How little value has been placed on the love of Christ! How little Christ's trust has profited Judas! Christ is worth but thirty pieces of silver to him. That was the price of a slave. Christ the Master is valued as a slave. Christ the friend – who measured all things in the light of love – is betrayed for about eighteen dollars by one who views all things in the light of material gain. Little wonder that the inspired Prophet puts these words into the mouth of Christ: "It is a handsome price that I was prized at by them" (Zach. 11:13).

Judas now approaches Christ. All the love in the great heart of Jesus goes out in one last offer of mercy to Judas. It is the only hope left for the unfortunate Apostle. Gently and sadly, Christ asks: "Friend, wherefore art thou come?" (Mt. 26:50.) Jesus knows this man is a hireling of His enemies. Jesus knows that he is the instigator of this ruffian mob. And still, with divine compassion, with infinite patience, with holy love, He calls this traitor – "Friend."

This charity of Christ is wasted. Judas is not moved. He draws near to Christ, *and he kisses Him.* It is the kiss of death. The most expressive mark of human love and respect is turned against the loving Christ. Had Judas struck the gentle Saviour, it would have wounded Him less. "Judas," our Blessed Lord cries out in tones that have made that name a byword for treachery, deceit, and hypocrisy for all time. "Judas!" How it must have pierced the soul of the ingrate who bore that name! "Judas, dost thou betray the Son of Man with a kiss?" (Lk. 23:48.)

This is a hard question for the gentle Christ to ask. It is a hard question for the treacherous Apostle to answer. There is no answer. Actions speak louder than words. Christ allows Himself to be taken prisoner by the mob. The bitterness of the agony in the Garden has begun to come to pass. Christ has been sold out. But He shall buy back thousands of souls on the morrow. Judas has a full purse – a bargain sale – but on the morrow he will perish as an outcast and as a madman with his very bowels burst asunder.

Look upon Christ as He is betrayed. Christ is noble because He is loyal. He was a loyal friend even to His worst enemy. Loyal friends have devotion toward one another. Loyal friends have wholehearted confidence and appreciation for each other.

When Christ was betrayed, a friend became disloyal to Him. A friend proved faithless and lacking in devotion. A friend proved himself unworthy of the trust which Christ had given him. A friend was so utterly lacking in appreciation of Christ that he valued Him at thirty pieces of tarnished silver.

Judas was disloyal in thought, in word, and in deed.

Let us, however, not condemn Judas. God is his judge. Rather let us look with compassion on Jesus. The betrayal by Judas, with a kiss, was only the first in a long series of acts in which the goods of this world have been preferred to Christ. People have given up the Faith for a better salary. Men have given up the Faith for bigger business opportunities. Women have betrayed Christ for a higher position on the social ladder.

The second hour of the day is the wakening hour. And what are our thoughts? In this day and age of materialism, our thoughts are usually on money matters.

Every day men start off with a mad rush for money. Money is the lifeblood of our civilization. People fear peril to their money more than peril to their lives. For example, atomic shelters for people are still in the discussion stage, while transit advertisements for commuters offer vaults to protect money and valuables against any kind of attack. "Money more than man," is a startling revelation.

More revealing yet, and more disheartening, is the preference that even Christians give money and material, over virtue and the salvation of their souls. Our Lord told us clearly that we ought to "Seek first the kingdom of God and his justice, and all other things shall be added unto you" (Lk. 12:31).

Christ is betrayed over and over again today. Yet He is still the model of loyalty and fidelity. Christ was loyal to His cause and to His friends unto the last drop of His precious blood.

Let us put first things first. Nothing shall be preferred to Christ. There is no necessity of this life that is worth the betrayal of Christ – even the whole world. "What doth it profit a man if he gain the whole world, or what exchange shall a man give for his soul?" (Mk. 8:36.)

Money is useful as a means to an end, and that end ought to be heaven. Money is useless as an end in itself. Its evil effect is always the same. It betrays Christ and destroys our life here and hereafter. Yesterday it was Judas — today read the daily press. The manner may change; the net result is the same. "And casting down the pieces of silver . . . he departed and going out, hanged himself with a halter" (Mt. 27:5).

How to Meditate Further on This Chapter

COMPOSITION OF PLACE

a) *Physical:* A band of ruffians enters the sleepy quiet of the garden. With lanterns, and staffs, and swords, and ropes they are seeking out the blessed Christ. They know Him not, but Judas the traitor is at their head to put the finger on his Master.

b) *Spiritual:* The Heart of Jesus is heavy with the thought of His own Apostle's treachery. He tries again to dissuade Judas from his crime. He calls him, "Friend." He asks him solemnly, "Whereunto art thou come?" He tries to prevent sin with love. To convey His own strength to a weak member.

WHO IS IT THAT SUFFERS?

This is the Good Shepherd of His flock. And one of His very own, like a wandering sheep, has turned away from Him. Like the shepherd who knows his own, Jesus is seeking him out.

WHAT DOES HE SUFFER?

a) *Spiritually:* He knows the value of a soul. He sees

one on the brink of destruction. He knows the value of grace. Here He sees it spurned. No one understands so well the dignity of the priesthood, of the Christian. Yet here an Apostle becomes an apostate. One whom He has chosen, chooses another Master to himself.

b) *Mentally:* Jesus has been betrayed for thirty pieces of silver. Money has been preferred to Him. He is rated less than this world's goods. With divine irony the thought comes to His mind through the Prophet Zachary, "It is a handsome price that I was prized at by them."

c) *Physically:* Christ's cheek is seared by the kiss of death. He is apprehended by the rough hands of cruel men. He is treated like a robber. Bound with cords. Pushed about. Made to stumble and drink perforce of the brook Cedron as He is led off to prison and to death.

WHY DOES HE SUFFER?

a) *Chronologically:* From disappointment. From being sold for the price of a slave. From disloyalty. From the treachery of a loved one. From the wasteful disregard of the hours spent in His company, the lessons learned at His feet, the warnings that proceeded from His lips.

b) *Mystically:* From the constant disregard of His love by sinners who sell Him out for thirty fleeting moments of stolen pleasure. From those who neglect grace. From my preference of others over Him. From my false sense of values. From my forgetfulness of His law. From my infidelity to my vocation. From my prizing Him too little, and loving sin and the dangers of sin too much.

WHAT AM I GOING TO DO ABOUT IT?

Resolutions: I shall remember the words of St. Peter, "He who commits sin, is the slave of sin." I shall not be made a slave of sin in the future. I shall not sell out Christ the Lord for the price of slavery. I shall be loyal to Him in thought, word, and deed. I shall realize it is better to have a thousand enemies than one friend who can cause me to betray Jesus. I cannot serve two masters.

PRAYER

O Lord Jesus Christ, who at the beginning of Thy Sacred Passion didst will to be betrayed by the traitor's kiss and sold for thirty pieces of silver, mercifully grant that we may always choose wisely those things which please Thee, and never forsake Thee for anything less. Who livest and reignest world without end. Amen.

ASPIRATION

"Jesus, meek and humble of heart, make our heart like unto Thine" (*500 days' indul.; Racc. No. 227*).

The Hour of Desertion

THREE o'clock is the hour of solitude and desertion. Even the brightness of modern lighting cannot enliven or dissipate the loneliness of deserted streets and the sightless sockets of darkened windows at that hour. The poet and dramatist have always sensed its desolation and have set it by the clock as the time for dark deeds of evil men.

In their miniatures and capitals for the third hour, the famous illuminators of the medieval hour books were sparing of gold leaf, the symbol of light and glory. Deep purples predominate and action pictures are rare.

In the history of the Passion of Jesus Christ, the third event worthy of note is the desertion of Him by His Apostles, who fled leaving Him alone. Thus the third hour of our Saviour's sufferings is the hour of abandonment. Jesus Christ, however, is true God as well as true man. Every hour is His. And every hour is His triumph.

The Holy Scripture describes the desertion of Christ as follows: "Then the disciples, all leaving Him, fled" (Mt. 27:56). At this time also were fulfilled the prophetic words of Zachary: "I will strike the shepherd and the sheep of the flock shall be dispersed" (Zach. 13:7).

In the gospel account of this shameful deed, we see that in the first place Jesus sought the welfare of the Apostles by voluntarily delivering Himself into the hands of His enemies, saying: "I have told you that I am he. If therefore you seek me let these go their way" (Jn. 18:8). Yet the solicitude of Jesus for the disciples had no kindred feeling in their own hearts, because on seeing the Master apprehended and bound they left Him.

A few words of the human tongue can only suggest the effect of an action on the human heart. The Apostles all left Jesus. Not one friend remained. The defection was complete. The Holy Ghost makes a distinction in the action of the Apostles, saying, "leaving him, they fled" (Mt. 27:56). Here in the first part we see the desertion, in their leaving Him. This leaving Christ was a spiritual act, an inward dissociation from Christ, an intellectual turning from Him. After the inward severance followed the outer one – they fled.

Even the agony was not so lonely. At least the exhausted and troubled sleep of the Apostles was involuntary and they remained physically present. Christ was then lonely but not alone. Now with free choice His chosen friends have alienated themselves from Him in their hearts and literally left Him to Himself.

This is a desolate hour, but not one that has come by surprise. Earlier that night, Jesus had warned His companions of what was to come. "All you shall be scandalized in me this night" (Mt. 26:31). But the disciples did not wish to believe this word. "Peter answering said to him, 'Although all shall be scandalized in thee, I will never be scandalized' " (Mt. 26:33). " 'Yea, though I should die

with thee, I will not deny thee.' And all the others said the same thing" (Mt. 26:35).

Even with divine warning, this came as a surprise to the Apostles. Their weakness was their surprise. For they all left and fled.

In keeping with our general background of the medieval hour books, we can see that the third hour was indeed a dark hour for Christ the God-Man. The prophet has put these words in His mouth, "I looked for one who would grieve together with me, but there was none; and I sought for one who would comfort me, and I found none" (Ps. 68:21). And again, "Thou hast put my acquaintance from me. . . . Friend and neighbor thou hast put far from me, and my acquaintance because of my misery" (Ps. 87:9, 19).

In our life today as individuals and as communities, we are surrounded by desertion and loneliness. How hard it is to understand the ease and thoughtlessness with which those upon whom we have depended can leave us. How hard this is especially in a time of need or sorrow. It is difficult to suffer at the hands of enemies, but the wound is deep and burning when it comes from a friend. Perhaps the only true sign, the only real test of a friend is his willingness to stand fast by us when we are afflicted, and the courage to sacrifice himself for another. Some friends are willing but do not carry through in their actions. Others never even get *that* far. Such was the case of the Apostles, who first left and then fled.

Our daily press is filled with stories of desertions of the most unnatural kind. Mothers who leave their families, small children at that, to seek entertainment elsewhere. These women have neither the willingness to stand fast nor the courage to sacrifice. They leave and then flee.

Husbands and wives, bound together by the deepest union of love in this world, who will not and do not live up to the marriage contract. How ridiculous it is for men and women who were unwilling to stand fast or to sacrifice themselves in one case, indeed often with all the helps of the very sacrament itself, to think that on a second or third marriage they will succeed.

Children in this day desert their parents. They forsake their spiritual Mother, Holy Church. Why? Because they have not the will to persevere or the courage to sacrifice.

Nations no longer trust one another. They bind themselves in solemn pacts. They build houses of glass to cherish the theory of these noble ideals. And what happens? The first time they are called upon to stand together, they leave, and they take flight.

Sworn friends among the nations who give testimony of their good will do not hesitate to sell instruments of death to mutual enemies. In so doing they have taken their leave. And their flight is inevitable.

Paradoxically, there is only one hero in a desertion; there is only one winner; only one who stands fast. It is he who was deserted. For those who leave and flee will leave again and again, and spend a weary lifetime in flight, unless they return to their first conqueror, him whom they deserted. This is the glory of Christ, that He was deserted. This is the glory of the Apostles that, after many leavings and many flights, they returned humble and repentant to Him from whom they had fled.

Perhaps nowhere in His Passion is our Blessed Lord more completely the Man of the Hour than in His hour of desolation and abandonment, because when forsaken by all He became the One to whom all must return at the peril of their souls.

It is this thought that should point the way for personal and international peace. Fear, guilt, loneliness, superiority and inferiority complexes which are the distraction of modern men and women, can be fully dissipated only in the return to Christ, the forsaken One. War, rumors of war, strife and dissent, suspicion and mistrust, will disappear from the international horizon only when Christ is sought out and clung to.

With the ancient Fathers of the Church, who commented on the seizure of Christ and the withdrawal of the Apostles, we can attribute this lonely hour of the Passion to these two ingenious manifestations of God's love for us. In the first place, Christ permitted the flight of His Apostles that He might suffer more for us and by this deeper drinking of the chalice of bitterness merit a more bountiful redemption for us. And, in the second place, to prepare the Apostles for the work of saving the world, by thus increasing their humility and disarming their confidence in their own strength.

The practical application is very simple. Like most simple things, however, the knack is hard to attain. Every time we come upon a lonely hour, we must realize it is a gift from God. A sharing in His Passion given to us for the same reasons as His own lonely hour. We are asked to endure this hard thing to increase our love for God, and to learn to lean on Him instead of on ourselves. We should seek heavenly assistance instead of human diversions. Beach resorts and mountain ranges fall far short of our own home if Christ be with us at home. The pause that refreshes, whether in the form of soft or hard drink, will have to be invoked again and again, unless Christ gives refreshment beyond all comprehension. "Whosoever drinketh of this water shall thirst again: but he that shall drink of the water that I will give him, shall not thirst forever.

"But the water that I will give him shall become in him a fountain of water, springing up into life everlasting" (Jn. 4:13).

How to Meditate Further on This Chapter

COMPOSITION OF PLACE

a) *Physical:* The Garden of Olives in the dead of night. Even the enemies of Christ have been confounded because He has struck them to the ground. There is no doubt about His power. No one can suspect weakness in Him. He defends the innocence of his followers and demands that they be set free. But instead of relying on Christ, on His word, on His manifest power, they leave Him and flee.

b) *Spiritual:* This action of the Apostles is a twofold sorrow to the heart of Christ. A poignant phase of the interior sufferings of Jesus. First His chosen ones leave Him. Then they take flight. They turn against Him first in their interior by turning their will against Him, and forgetting who He is and what He can do. Then they perform an external act of running away. Christ is truly deserted in this hour, even by those whom He has defended.

WHO IS IT THAT SUFFERS?

This is the Son of God who tells us without any equivocation, "I am the Way, the Truth, and the Life." Those who leave Him are lost for they are not in the Way that leads to salvation. Those who flee from Him are in the deepest error, for they have forsaken the Truth. Those who desert Him, are dead, for they have preferred death to Life itself.

WHAT DOES HE SUFFER?

a) *Spiritually:* There is a deep sense of abandonment in the soul of the Blessed Christ. So deep that the Psalmist exclaims in His name, "I looked for one who would grieve together with me, but there was none; and I sought for one who would comfort me, and I found none" (Ps. 68:21). Sometimes we feel happy alone. Often solitude is our choice. But here in the garden at the beginning of His Passion, Christ wanted a friend to be His consolation and all, leaving Him, fled.

b) *Physically:* Precisely because those He trusted have left Him, Jesus is now left alone in the hands of His enemies. Not one kind face. Not one helping hand. Not one encouraging word. The last drops of human kindness are denied Him. His is the worst kind of loneliness . . . alone in a crowd. He is surrounded by uninterested spectators. No one cares how He feels. He knows that His misery is a matter of indifference to those about Him.

c) *Mentally:* The sorrows of our dear Lord are increased in measure because He remembers that He had warned the disciples and they would not heed Him. He recalls their vain protests, "Yea though I should die with thee, I will not deny thee" (Mt. 26:35). He knows that He has seen the last of most of them until after the bitterness of His death and burial has given way to the hope of the Resurrection.

WHY DOES HE SUFFER?

a) *Chronologically:* From the ache of loneliness. From

the disgrace of being a deserted leader. From the knowledge that those He loves think more of themselves than they do of Him. The Hosannas of Sunday are lost in the lonely silence of Thursday night.

b) *Mystically:* From all the desertions of all the ages. From the endless number who have left Him, and then run away. From all the chosen souls who tire of His service, forget His power, His promises, and His warnings. From the number of defections in the ranks of the holy priesthood. From the number of religious who have lost their vocations. From the bad marriages. The broken homes. The Christians who follow their own will rather than God's. For every poor sinner who has left Christ, and does not return but continues to run away. He suffers because I have left Him out of my life. Because I have deserted Him. Because I deceive myself He no longer cares for me, forgetful of the adage, "If thou art further from God today, than thou wast yesterday, remember it is not God who has moved."

WHAT AM I GOING TO DO ABOUT IT?

Resolutions: I will remember the presence of God. I shall remind myself that no matter where I go, nor with whom I associate, nor what I do, God is my witness, as well as my Judge. I will respect His presence about me, within me, and in my neighbor. I shall so act as to be always ready to give an account of myself to Him, that I may never be separated from Him by sin. I will try to see His will in all things. I will prefer His will to mine.

PRAYER

O Lord Jesus Christ, true Shepherd of my soul, struck

by Thine enemies, and deserted by Thy sheep, give me the will and the strength never to be separated from Thee, and to walk always in company with Thee on earth, that we may dwell together forever in heaven. Who livest and reignest world without end. Amen.

ASPIRATION

"Sweet Heart of Jesus, have mercy on us and on our erring brethren" (*300 days' indul.; Racc. No. 233*).

The Hour of Injustice

IT IS the dark hour of the morning. A tall, pale man is hurried off into the dead of night for trial, imprisonment, and torture. Armed guards take Him by night for fear of the people. His enemies dare not take Him by day. They watched Him, looking for a fault, and found none. He taught daily in the temple but they did not apprehend Him.

His enemies try to make Him confess all manner of false deeds. Testimony is brought against Him. He is judged guilty before His trial. Falsehood, intrigue, wounded pride, and hatred for God have all coalesced in His condemnation, and in the dark hour a curtain is drawn over His trial and separates the innocent one from His friends.

Who is this man? His name is legion. When did this happen? Yesterday, today, and tomorrow. Jesus Christ is the Man of the Hour. And every hour is His triumph. From His first triumph over false trials, He has been conquering falsehood and intrigue and hatred of God in His Church. Pope Boniface VIII, Pope Pius VII; Cardinal Fisher, Cardinal Mindszenty; Archbishop St. Thomas à Becket, Archbishop Stepinac; the modern martyrs of Mexico and China continue in time the history of the false trials of their suffering Saviour who foretold this succession of persecution and injustice.

"If you had been of the world, the world would love its own: but because you are not of the world, but I have chosen you out of the world, therefore the world hateth you. If they have persecuted me, they will also persecute you" (Jn. 15:19).

The story of the Passion describes simply the arrest and seizure of Jesus Christ. "Then the band and the tribune, and the servants of the Jews took Jesus and bound him, and they led him away to Annas first, for he was the father-in-law to Caiphas, who was the high priest of that year" (Jn. 18:12).

The medieval illuminators portray Christ as bound with ropes and chains as He is led from the Garden to Annas. He was violently goaded on by His captors and, weakened as He was from loss of blood in the Agony, He fell many times. Many commentators believe that at this time the gentle Saviour even fell into the brook of Cedron. "He shall drink of the torrent on the way" (Ps. 109:7). Christ was led into the city through the Golden Gate which was called the Sheep's Gate.

The first stop was at the house of Annas. This hoary politician, according to Josephus, had obtained for himself the dignity of High Priest by bribing the Roman governor. In the course of time his son-in-law and four of his sons also obtained this office, the youngest, when Annas was ninety. His great influence was due to his malicious tongue and tremendous wealth.

Why was Christ brought to this old rogue, who had no authority over Him? St. John gives us the first reason.

Annas was the father-in-law of the High Priest, and such a consideration for the father-in-law would surely set the chief priests in well with the son-in-law. Both the Acts of the Apostles (4:6) and St. Cyril of Alexandria point to Annas as the very soul of the whole conspiracy against Christ. It was with Annas that Judas had bargained.

Annas takes advantage of this visit from Jesus to question Him about His disciples and His works. But Jesus is silent. Annas, a judge without right, needles with more insistence concerning Christ's doctrine. Then Jesus silences Annas and covers him with confusion when He says: "I have spoken openly to the world. I have always taught in the synagogue and in the temple, whither all the Jews resort; and in secret I have spoken nothing. Why asketh thou me? Ask them who have heard what I have spoken unto them. Behold they know what things I have said" (Jn. 18:20).

What a blow are these words to the pride of the scheming ancient. In a single statement Christ has laid bare all his spying and prying by simply telling him to check again with his agents. This dignified answer of Christ so enrages and confuses the false judge that he is speechless.

Actions speak louder than words, and one of the servants standing by gives Jesus a blow on the face, saying, "Answerest thou the high Priest so?" (Jn. 18:22.)

This blow in the face is a public insult, grievous in intent and effect. It is the thought that the servant who struck Jesus was an armed guard that induced the artists of the ages of faith to represent him with a mailed fist, the armored glove of ancient times. Thus, even till now, the mailed fist is an emblem of the Passion.

The reaction of Jesus to this outrage is transcendent, rising above the rage of His judge, the violence of His attacker, and the prejudice of the bystanders, as He gently replies: "If I have spoken evil, give testimony of the evil; but if well, why strikest thou me?" (Jn. 18:23.)

This time there is no answer. Guilt has silenced all. Embarrassed, Annas sends Jesus away bound, to Caiphas the High Priest.

Now begins the second false trial of Christ. This is one of the foulest miscarriages of justice in human records. A sacred tribunal endowed with religious as well as juridical authority was used as a tool for deicide. St. John Chrysostom says of this second false trial of Jesus, "It presented only the appearance of a court; in reality it was an assault of robbers."

This trial was false and unjust in every detail. It was false and unjust in the time at which it was held. According to the law, even the sacred body of the Sanhedrin was not to hold a trial at night, nor could a man be condemned to death during the night.

The intention of the trial was false and unjust. The judges had already decided on the death sentence for Jesus and the hearing was to be a formality only. The witnesses were false. There were no witnesses in favor of Jesus. None came forth, and if they had they would have been accused as accomplices. When the false witnesses were brought forth, they contradicted one another, as David had foretold. "Unjust witnesses have risen up against me; and iniquity hath lied to itself" (Ps. 26:12).

When the High Priest saw what a fiasco the trial was developing into, he rose up and thundered: "Answerest thou nothing to the things which these witnesses prefer against thee?" (Mt. 26:62.)

But Jesus was silent. Nothing had to be said, for all the accusations were patently trumped up charges.

Then the High Priest said to Him, "I adjure thee by the living God that thou tell us if thou be the Christ the Son of God" (Mt. 26:63).

This was an astute question. No matter what answer was given, Caiphas had a lever for condemning Jesus. If Jesus said no, Caiphas would condemn Him as a liar, claimant of a dignity not His. If He said yes, He could be called a blasphemer.

Jesus made answer and the Accused became the Judge. "Thou hast said it. Nevertheless I say to you hereafter you shall see the Son of Man sitting on the right hand of the power of God and coming in the clouds of heaven" (Mt. 26:64).

Then the High Priest, with dramatic hypocrisy, ripped his sacerdotal vestments and cried out, "He hath blasphemed. What further need have we of witnesses? Behold now you have heard the blasphemy. What think you?" But they answered and said: "He is guilty of death" (Mt. 26:66). This is the end of the second false trial of our Lord. Justice has not only been blindfolded but torn limb from limb.

"Then did they spit in his face, and buffeted him" (Mt. 26:67). Here is the peak of the hatred so open in the trial of Jesus. We are told by some of the ancient historians, that it was the custom of the times, and indeed the usual practice, for the judges to rise from their seats of judgment after they had pronounced the death sentence and spit in the face of the condemned. According to the testimony of the Evangelist, we see that this usage was vehemently complied with at the trial of Christ.

As the judges left the hall they struck our Lord and

gave wicked example to the soldiers and servants. It is amazing that when well-educated and prominent people, men with authority and position, abandon religion and morality they excel even the rabble in brutality. The events of Christ's Passion show this. The history of the French Revolution and modern reprisals of war prove that this proclivity is still alive.

The false trials of Jesus and their modern counterparts must fill this generation with astonishment and fear. With wonder, that the machinery of justice, man's share in the Divine Justice and his hope for human rights, can so readily be made the tool of evil men, and so rapidly descend to hypocrisy. With fear, that this instrument of freedom may yet be turned into a mailed fist to strike the innocent.

The only way justice can perdure is when the law is loved, respected, and observed. We must begin with the Ten Commandments. The law of God should be honored once more in the American home. Children should again be taught respect for authority and the love of truth. Schools should accentuate the obligation of keeping the law and of upholding it, rather than the ways of defrauding it.

True justice and real jurisprudence are dispensed by men to men. Those trained in this science have a weighty obligation. In our day we see those who connive at breaking the law and overthrowing justice, fly to the shadow of the law and scream about infringement of their rights. But those who administer justice should do so without fear. They must imitate Christ.

Christ died because He loved the law of God. He died to save us from the punishment men were under from the law. He died that men might love the law and live under it. His own false trial is as new as tomorrow's headline. This generation cannot afford to miss this lesson from the Passion of Jesus Christ. "Blessed are ye, when they shall revile you, and persecute you, and speak all that is evil against you, untruly, for my sake: Be glad and rejoice" (Mt. 5:11). "Seek ye first the kingdom of God and his justice and all other things will be added unto you" (Lk. 12:31).

How to Meditate Further on This Chapter

COMPOSITION OF PLACE

a) *Physical:* Consider in your mind's eye the two courtrooms of the false trials. The homes of Annas and of Caiphas. The darkest hour of the night. The enemies of Christ awake and waiting to ensnare Him.

b) *Spiritual:* The God who is Truth is on trial. Justice Itself is faced with the injustice of men. The very ones who should have known better, who sat in the chair of Moses, whose life was the law, are now about to ignore the law, defy the traditions of the ancients, and themselves blaspheme against the Son of God.

WHO IS IT THAT SUFFERS?

This is the Judge of the world to come. This is our true High Priest, the only mediator between God and men, Christ Jesus, the Son of God. He is now made a scapegoat. His word is scorned, but He is still the Truth Itself. God of God, Light of Light, True God of True God.

WHAT DOES HE SUFFER?

a) *Spiritually:* He suffers in the blasphemy of those

who try to make of God a deceiver. He suffers because those who are leaders of the people turned against Him out of envy. He suffers in the thought of all innocent men who have ever or will ever suffer unjustly.

b) *Mentally:* He suffers from the false witnesses who change the meaning of His words, vitiate His charity, question His truthfulness, and accuse Him of rebelling against the law, which He had come to fulfill. He suffers from the pride of His judges, the arrogance of His accusers, and the malice of His enemies who gloat over His capture and undoing.

c) *Physically:* Jesus suffers from being tightly bound after His arrest. From having fallen into the brook Cedron as He was roughly pushed to trial. He suffers from a blow in the face with the mailed fist of the servant of the High Priest. He suffered from being blindfolded. From being buffeted. From being spat upon. From being pushed and juggled off to solitary confinement in this dark hour of injustice.

WHY DOES HE SUFFER?

a) *Chronologically:* He suffers injustice in time that Justice may reign eternally. He suffers to show the innocent how to suffer. He suffers in His reputation, in His body, in His authority, and in His material possessions to show us that the true purpose of life cannot be found in these things. He fears not those who kill the body, but He suffers to encourage all men to suffer for justice and for truth.

b) *Mystically:* He suffers for my injustice toward my neighbor. For my rash judgments. For my gossip. For my calumny and detraction. For my unwillingness to listen to the truth or to change my mind even when I know I am wrong. He suffers for my sins of anger, cursing, swearing, and blasphemy. For my lack of respect for God, and His church, and His law, and things holy.

WHAT AM I GOING TO DO ABOUT IT?

Resolutions: To honor God's name, and never use it lightly or in vain. To respect all holy persons, places, and things. To tell the truth even though I shall suffer for it. To make restitution when I am the cause of my neighbor losing his good name. To restrain my anger and to watch my words.

PRAYER

O Lord Jesus Christ, led as a Lamb to the slaughter, and silent in the face of false accusers and unjust judges, grant we beseech Thee, that we who follow after Thee, may know the truth, love the truth, and follow the truth in all meekness and patience who livest and reignest forever. Amen.

ASPIRATION

Sweetest Jesus, be not my Judge, but my Saviour (*300 days' indul.; Racc. No. 71*).

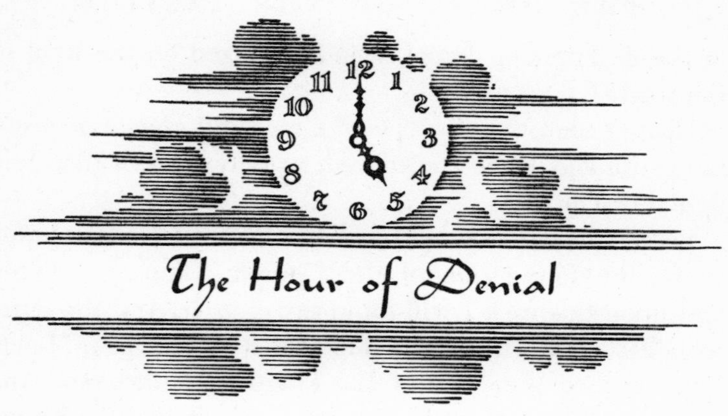

THE fifteenth-century Crusaders' Hymn, *Schönster Herr Jesus,* ends with the words, "One only glance, for me were bliss untold." The reference is to the divine efficacy of a single glance from the gentle Christ. These soldiers of the cross kept up their lagging spirits with this joyful paean.

In this history of the Passion of Jesus, there is a marvelous confirmation of the power of a single look from the eyes of our Saviour. Our Blessed Lord, after His false trial and ignominious treatment at the hands of Annas and Caiphas and their minions, is led off to prison. In the midst of His own sorrow, He does not forget Peter, weighed down with the guilt of three denials. "And the Lord turning looked upon Peter" (Lk. 22:61).

The salutary effect of Christ's loving glance at Peter is described by our Lord Himself: "I have prayed for thee that thy faith fail not; and thou being once converted, confirm thy brethren" (Lk. 22:32). St. Jerome explains further, "If even the eye of a mother has power to conquer hearts, it was impossible for him (Peter) to remain in the darkness of denial, who had gazed on the light of the world."

Having seen the effects of the merciful glance of Jesus, the cause should be considered, namely, Peter's threefold denial of Christ.

Peter, of all the associates of the Redeemer, was chosen to be the foundation of the Church. "Thou art Peter, and upon this rock I will build my church. And the gates of hell shall not prevail against it" (Mt. 16:18). "I will give to thee the keys of the kingdom of heaven. And whatsoever thou shalt bind upon earth, it shall be bound also in heaven; and whatsoever thou shalt loose on earth, it shall be loosed also in heaven" (Mt. 16:19).

Peter was indeed a rock. He was a born leader. The kind of man who can give orders and have everyone follow him without question. The kind of man who could state his own opinion clearly and definitely and confidently make his cause their own.

Like most people with his qualities of leadership, confidence, and decision, Peter was hasty, impatient, and intolerant of others. Yet Peter had a great heart; he was capable of intense love, ready to forgive and quick to repent.

No one understood Peter better than our Blessed Lord — none was more appreciative of his earnest love, deep sincerity, and disarming candor. Peter's weaknesses of character were such that, given the proper direction and supernatural assistance, they could be and were actually turned into great assets for God, for the Church, and for his own salvation.

The prince of the Apostles had merited not only our Lord's special selection but also His special attention. The Master had warned Simon Peter frequently of

dangers in store for both of them. On one occasion, we see the stubborn Apostles roundly rebuked for lack of understanding.

"Jesus began to show his disciples that he must go to Jerusalem and suffer many things from the ancients and Scribes and chief priests, and be put to death, and the third day rise again. And Peter, taking him, began to rebuke him saying, Lord, be it far from thee, this shall not be unto thee. Who turning, said to Peter: Go behind me, Satan: Thou art a scandal unto me, because thou savourest not the things that are of God, but the things that are of men" (Mt. 16:21–23).

But Peter seems to have forgotten the warnings of Jesus. He continued as the leader and spokesman for the Apostolic band. He paid the taxes. He even went so far as to have our Lord perform a family miracle for him in curing the illness of his mother-in-law.

Certainly not in the maudlin, puerile manner of the unrecognizable Christ of *The Nazarene,* but in a spirit of courteous companionability, our Lord had come to rely on Peter. Peter was gratified; he was elated; his expansive nature became even more enveloping and protective. Finally, at the Last Supper, when the foreknowledge of His Passion, already begun, lowered over the occasion, Jesus had the opportunity to warn Peter three times to take care lest his overconfidence lead to ruin.

The Saviour told His disciples that He was about to leave them and that none of them at this time could follow, but they would surely follow hereafter. Peter, feeling left out, exclaimed, "Why cannot I follow thee now? I will lay down my life for thee. Lord, I am ready to go with thee both to prison and to death" (Jn. 13:36).

The God-Man again clearly foretold events. "You will

all be scandalized in my regard this night" (Mt. 26:31).

Peter again objected, "Although all shall be scandalized in thee, I will never be scandalized in thee" (Mt. 26:32).

Besides the two general warnings, Jesus now makes a third very pointed one for the benefit of Peter alone. "Amen I say to thee, that in this night before the cock crow thou wilt deny me thrice" (Mt. 26:34).

Peter, forgetting himself, answered: "Yea, though I should die with thee I will not deny thee" (Mt. 26:35). And all the rest, taking their cue from Peter and not the Lord, made answer and said the same thing.

Events happened quickly and suddenly. Peter ran away with a bloody sword in his grasp. Shame and humiliation forced him to retrace his steps and find out how things went with the Master. On the way he met John, who had access to the house of Caiphas. He entered into the courtyard, where his uneasy manner called attention to himself. A maid-servant, probably recognizing Peter as the constant companion of Jesus, came up to him and declared, "Thou also wast with Jesus the Galilean."

"But he denied before them all, saying, I know not what thou sayest" (Mt. 26:70).

Another serving woman made the same observation. Again Peter denied Jesus, and with an oath.

"And after a little while, they came that stood by and said to Peter: Surely thou art one of them. For even thy speech doth discover thee. Then he began to curse and to swear that he knew not the man. And immediately the cock crew" (Mt. 26:73–74).

Here, one after another in rapid succession, were the denials which Jesus had foretold. How easy it is to go from one sin to another. St. Gregory gives the explanation.

"Sin, when not removed by penance, by its very own weight soon drags down to another sin."

But Jesus Christ is the Man of the Hour. Every hour is His triumph. At the hour of the cock crow, He is led from the hall of injustice through the fire-lit courtyard to prison. And in the flash of an eye, He reduces the proud Apostle to a humble disciple and makes the quitter into a penitent confessor.

"And going forth Peter wept bitterly" (Mt. 26:75).

The medieval hour books abound with imagery for the hour of Peter's denial and Christ's conquest. The rooster, the servantmen, and the maids leer at Peter. Peter is shown with a copious handkerchief. And not infrequently the glance of Jesus is represented by a great tearful eye. It is thus amazing that with childlike simplicity the artists of the ages of Faith could put their finger on the cause and the effect of the denial. The occasion was bad companions. Had Peter stayed with St. John, he would not have laid himself open to temptation. But, instead, he drew near to the fire, feeling worse for himself than for Jesus. Why did he seek out Christ's enemies? Why did he converse with them? Peter's undoing was seeking creature comforts in his sorrow, instead of having recourse to God.

Many Christians today follow Peter's weakness, rather than his immediate repentance. The secularism of our day is leading people farther from God and nearer the fire, with their "one religion is as good as another" attitude. As a result of this we see tolerance bending over backward in civil relationships and an increase of mixed marriages. Even some of those who are supposed to be the elite of our faith, Catholic college graduates, give all kinds of explanations why they can keep company with those outside the Church. What shall we say of those parents who deny Catholic education to the young for purely social reasons? How can our teen-agers advance in virtue when they are allowed the complete freedom of neglect to wander away from God to the edge of the fire?

This generation may not be granted the same grace as Peter. Nor can we be sure that the reaction will be the same instant conversion to Christ and lifelong penitence and sorrow for the denial of Christ. There is a well-established tradition regarding the sorrow of Peter. It was so great and so constant that the cheeks of the first pope were actually furrowed by his holy tears. His life of penance, zeal, and mortification is well known, even to his crucifixion upside down because he esteemed himself unworthy to die the same way as Jesus had died.

And then we have the mystery of the holy glance of Christ. Perhaps there is no better explanation of this saving look of Jesus than the words of the spouse, the loving soul, in the Canticle of Canticles. "Thou hast wounded my heart, my spouse: Thou hast wounded my heart with one of thy eyes" (Cant. 4:9).

How to Meditate Further on This Chapter

COMPOSITION OF PLACE

a) *Physical:* The courtyard of the High Priest. It is in the dead of night. It is cold. There is a great fire with men and women warming themselves about it. At any moment Christ the Lord will pass through the courtyard on His way to imprisonment. Peter is waiting for Him. But Peter is thinking of himself. He seeks creature comfort and is undone. But Jesus converts Him with one glance of mercy.

b) *Spiritual:* The denials of Peter wound the heart of Jesus excessively. This because they could have been so easily avoided. If only Peter had listened to Christ's warning. If only Peter had trusted in God and not himself. Yet here was Christ's "other self," His vicar on earth, seeking the warmth of earthly firesides and human companionship, and denying Christ the Lord. From anyone else, the wound would have been less. And the cry of the cock is one of misery for Peter and sharp disappointment for our loving Saviour.

WHO IS IT THAT SUFFERS?

Christ the Lord. The most loyal of all friends. The most respected of all Masters. The most beloved of all Lords. In Him there is no cooling of love. No thought of self. In Him there is no denial of His own. No shadow of turning. He is the constant lover.

WHAT DOES HE SUFFER?

a) *Spiritually:* He suffers in the knowledge that He cannot depend even on Peter the rock. He sees Himself denied because Peter seeks creatures and in his weakness is willing to settle for far less than God. He suffers because no heed was paid to His warnings. Because His friend is weak when he should have been strong. Because Peter's self-confidence has been his undoing. And because he put his own embarrassment above the truth which is Christ Himself.

b) *Physically:* Jesus knew it was Peter's love and good will that made him follow Christ even into the midst of His enemies. And this good will was some small measure of comfort. Yet even this little is deprived Him when Peter denies Him again, and again, and again. How often will this scene be repeated, when men will think more of themselves than of the sufferings of Christ. Now He is completely alone. Left to His tormentors. Abandoned by His own. With not even one strong friend to stand beside Him.

c) *Mentally:* The sorrow of the Son of Man is increased when He is mindful of how He warned Peter of the danger, and yet Peter would not listen. It is multiplied when He thinks of what drove Peter to this crime. A little fire. Jovial companionship. The needling of a servant maid. For desire of this little . . . and for fear of this nameless woman . . . Peter the rock has melted into wax in the hands of Satan. His bragging and loose promises have led him to denial of the One whom he loved, and who in return loves him.

WHY DOES HE SUFFER?

a) *Chronologically:* From the lack of faith that was put in His words. From the weakness of one who should have been strong. From Peter's preference of self and forgetfulness of the Passion. From Peter's unwarranted fear. From His own loneliness and abandonment. From the thought that even the last hope of consolation from His own has faded.

b) *Mystically:* Our Saviour suffers from my pride. From my confidence in self. From my lack of appreciation of His many warnings. From my love of the world and every creature comfort. From my desire to have God and everything else besides. From my turning after creatures. From my fear and lack of fortitude. From my forgetting Him. From my not co-operating with His graces as He so often looks upon me with mercy and forgiveness, while I hide from the look of His countenance.

WHAT AM I GOING TO DO ABOUT IT?

Resolutions: I will try and seek first the kingdom of God. I will avoid worldly companions, worldly distractions and amusements. I will look upon Jesus in His sufferings and beg His grace to overcome myself. I will often repeat the prayer of Peter after the Passion: "Lord, Thou knowest all things, Thou knowest that I love Thee."

PRAYER

O Lord Jesus Christ, abandoned and denied by Thy own in the midst of Thy bitter Passion, give me the grace to behold Thy adorable face, which so ravished the heart of Peter, and fix deeply within me Thy divine image, so that I may do Thy will on earth, and may be made worthy to come to the contemplation of Thy glorious face in heaven. Who livest and reignest forever. Amen.

ASPIRATION

"O Heart of love, I put all my trust in Thee; for I fear all things from my own weakness, but I hope all things from Thy goodness" (*300 days' indul.; Racc. No. 232*).

The Hour of Loneliness

ONE of the stormiest scenes in the Passion of Christ which both modern art and literature have altogether neglected is the imprisonment of Jesus Christ. There is no dearth of paintings of the *Ecce Homo,* or Christ before Pilate after His mistreatment by the Roman soldiers. From Fra Angelico and the medieval miniaturists, however, till the present, the sufferings of Christ at the hands of the Jews from the time of His trial to the Court of Pilate have been either forgotten or confused with later sufferings in Passion art.

This was the loneliest hour for the God-Man in His entire Passion. His false trial before the High Priest ended with the judges spitting in the face of Christ and walking out on Him, leaving our Saviour to the *gentle* care of the soldiers and servants of the High Priest. It is not surprising to see in the inspired narrative of the Passion that these menials continued to follow the despicable example of their masters.

St. Luke describes the scene for us. "And the men that held Jesus mocked him and struck him. And they blindfolded him and smote his face. And they asked him saying: Prophesy, Who is it that struck thee? And blaspheming, many other things they said against him" (Lk. 22:63).

This was what went on after Jesus had been led from His trial, through the courtyard where He healed Peter with a glance, and dragged into His prison to await the daylight. It was well that the prison of Jesus was subterranean. It was not becoming that the face of the earth should be defiled with such an orgy of wickedness and injustice. St. John Chrysostom tells us, "On that night, all the pits of the infernal world were unlocked, and after breaking their chains and the bolts of hell, Lucifer and his satellites rushed to Jerusalem, entered in and took possession of the bodies of all, Jews and pagans alike, to pour out through them upon Christ their long-stored hatred, envy, and anger, their rage, and all their fury." Surely a dramatic passage but not equal to the reality of that awful hour.

The remains of the low-vaulted, little prison in which Jesus was incarcerated still exist for the spectator to behold and be astonished. The niche for the earthen lamp reminds us of the lateness of the hour of the imprisonment of our Lord. He must have been half dead for the want of sleep and rest. He is fatigued by loss of blood in the Agony, by the stages of His forced march from the garden, and by the seemingly endless time He has been standing for false trials and abuse.

But Christ is not allowed a moment's rest. Indignity upon indignity is heaped upon our gentle Saviour. Our Lord is chained as a common criminal. Then He is made the sport of His jailers. They cover His face with a veil, half in jest for the mock prophet, and half in earnest, because they cannot stand the piteous gaze of the Man

of Sorrows. They strike Him. He is kicked and buffeted. They strike Him with rods or sticks and He is spat upon. These mad men even pluck the hair from His head and beard.

In this frightful abuse of Jesus is fulfilled the words the Prophet of old had put in the mouth of the Messias. "I have given over my body to the strikers, and my cheeks to them that plucked them. I have not turned away my face from them that rebuked me, and spit upon me" (Isa. 50:6).

They mock Jesus in His office of Prophet, striking Him beneath the filthy veil and asking Him to identify them who struck Him. And, sad to say, this divine descendant of Prophets and Kings did identify His strikers, reading their hearts and souls.

As if these words and deeds were not enough, they begin to blaspheme. Now they insult Jesus in His eternal office as the Son of God. What a shock to the gentle ears and Sacred Heart of Jesus. And Jesus weeps not for His sufferings but for the insults offered His heavenly Father and His own divinity.

"Weeping he hath wept in the night, and his tears are on his cheeks; there is none to comfort him among all them that were so dear to him: all his friends have despised him and become his enemies" (Lam. 1:16).

St. Athanasius warns the jailers of Christ, "Know you not that you are merely wounding your hands, while you strike the cornerstone?" While this apostrophe is eminently true, it does not detract from the inhuman and merciless treatment of Jesus Christ in His imprisonment.

To the medieval mind this treatment of Christ was almost incredible. The Passion miniatures represent Christ surrounded by a pack of jackals or hyenas. Again in an ancient manuscript from southern Germany, Jesus is represented behind bars with an iron collar about His neck, a kind of aureole of hands surrounding Him, and in almost cryptic medieval German the legend reads, "God in Distress."

What a soul-piercing thought! What a revelation to all those who love Jesus. God is in distress. In distress at the hands of impious men while He Himself is helpless, shackled, and imprisoned. This is indeed a bitter hour for Christ. A lonely and unforgettable hour. But Jesus Christ is the Man of the Hour. Every hour is His triumph. And even in this lonely hour He is the Conqueror.

Daybreak finds its way into the grated, sunken chamber and cruciform shadows fall upon the sleepless and blood-stained eyes of Jesus. The Saviour looks up, and with joy salutes the day for which He was born and for which He came into the world. With infinite tenderness He thanks His Father for this day of days. "His going forth is as the morning light" (Os. 6:3).

Most of us have lonely hours. Men and women have hours of distress, physical, mental, and spiritual. Our modern generation is in a prison of its own making—forced underground by its own fears. Even our song writers who seem to grasp the public pulse chant out, "Don't Fence Me In." What makes modern man the captive of his own circumstances? The answer lies in his fear of suffering. Afraid to suffer himself, man is now afflicted with medicinitis. From Adam, the way to sleep was to rise early, work hard, and retire at night tired. Today the night is turned into the day. The day is spent piling up nervous energy and a bottle of pills puts us to sleep at night. Modern men and women are amateur heart specialists, psychiatrists, cancer diagnosticians. The radio and television advertisements make healthy people a group of nervous, enervated, and expectant hospital cases. In their effort to prevent physical suffering in their bodies, they slip into nervous and mental suffering, the like of which past generations would never have imagined possible.

So-called advanced education would spare children suffering by letting them do as they want. Such a procedure merely puts off the reality of suffering until it will hurt them far more because they are not prepared for it.

The sufferings of old age are to be dissolved by a social security number, all planned out to make things easy for men. God's will and God's Providence are an unknown quantity as far as the bright lights of this world are concerned. But they are the only answers man has to suffering.

Not only artists and writers have overlooked the mistreatment of Jesus Christ in prison awaiting His trial. Christians have forgotten its lesson, the fact that even the earth itself is but a waiting station for the great trial, whether or not they are worthy of the kingdom of heaven. They are not without the means of salvation in the sacramental effects of the sufferings of Jesus and in utilizing their own personal sufferings. The precious example of our dear Lord in the sufferings during His imprisonment should be our best help in affliction and distress. Jesus Christ did not hide from suffering. It was His persecutors who blindfolded Him and threw a veil over His face.

St. Thomas tells us that in His Passion the Saviour endured every kind of suffering, physical, mental, and spiritual. He suffered in His body, in His soul, in His good name, in His offices, and from falsehood, injustice, and loneliness. At one time or other such sufferings in varying degree may come to the followers of Christ. During such times the thought not only of how much Jesus suffered for us but also the manner in which He suffered ought to set the pace for His disciples. They in their turn should imitate the quiet dignity of Jesus in the face of opposition and make their own the patient forbearance and the lack of personal retaliation and reprisal which He manifested to the great astonishment of His jailers.

St. Jerome tells us that the full narrative of all Jesus endured in the dark hours of His imprisonment will be revealed only on the day of judgment. Meanwhile the memory of this loneliest of hours in the Passion should be kept constantly before the mind and hearts of those who love Him. No one can ever feel alone or unloved after meditating on the sufferings of Jesus in prison. Those who are sick, those who are confined by age or circumstances, those who are alone and neglected, all have in Jesus, the Prisoner of love, a perfect model. No amount of money, no professional visits of charity, no joyful radio message, can bring the strength of will, the peace of soul, and the fullness of love that the message of the imprisoned Redeemer can give. "I am the Lord, thy God, who take thee by the hand, and say to thee: Fear not, I have helped thee" (Isa. 41:13).

How to Meditate Further on This Chapter

COMPOSITION OF PLACE

a) *Physical:* After His trial our Blessed Lord was imprisoned to await the convenience of His enemies in bringing Him before Pilate. The prison according to tradition was a small, damp subterranean cell. There was a little niche on the side for a lamp. Here the soldiers of the High Priest continue to buffet and make sport of Jesus Christ. And because of the beauty of His gaze, at once gentle, yet terrifying to those who abused Him, they cover the face of God with a blindfold.

b) *Spiritual:* Consider how sinful men try to hide from the face of God. Even when they abuse Him by their sins. The Heart of Jesus imprisoned and awaiting the death sentence is grieved by those who are so foolish as to think they can flee "from the wrath that is to come." Christ is surrounded by people but this is His hour of loneliness.

WHO IS IT THAT SUFFERS?

Here is the good God, who did not wish man to be alone. Who gave him a companion. Who praised those who would gather together even in small numbers of two or three in His name. Who gave man a social conscience and a desire to share. And in this hour He is alone. Here is the God who gave man freedom of will, freedom of action, freedom of the world, and He is imprisoned in a damp cellar hidden in the earth.

WHAT DOES HE SUFFER?

a) *Spiritually:* He suffers the loneliness of the innocent. The feeling that He alone is doing what is right. He suffers the loneliness of the just, persecuted as He is for justice' sake. He endures the loneliness of all those who must wait judgment. The sick who wait for the physician's answer. The accused who must await the decision of the court. The maligned, who must wait for time to justify the truth of their position. Those about to die, who must wait for the hand of God. Jesus is lonely in His heart and soul.

b) *Physically:* Jesus is left to the hands of an unruly band of paid ruffians who take their cue from their masters. If the High Priest could spit upon Him, why not they? If the servant could strike Him with a mailed fist and suffer no consequence, why not they? If all could mock Him, then He was fair game for them. He was therefore struck, mocked, spat upon, defiled and when His searching gaze made His attackers uncomfortable, He was blindfolded.

c) *Mentally:* Our Lord suffers here that men should think it so easy to hide themselves and their actions from God. That men should feel that because "everyone else is doing it" it is all right for them to follow suit. That because others can get away with something, all can be free with impunity. He suffers because no one will defend His honor. He suffers because none will recognize Him. He suffers because those He loves have turned against Him. Because His love is returned with the hatred of men.

WHY DOES HE SUFFER?

a) *Chronologically:* He suffers loneliness in time that He may share the kingdom of heaven forever with all men. He suffers at the hands of servants, that He may teach us that He is the Master of all. He allows His face to be covered from the sight of men that we may recognize Him as God veiled in humanity and suffering for us. He allows Himself to be imprisoned so that we may be made free.

b) *Mystically:* Jesus suffers for the number of times

I have neglected Him. He is mocked because so often I prefer others to Him. He is struck because by my sins I have buffeted Him. He is blindfolded because I have tried in vain to hide from His sight. He suffers for all those who will ever fall into the hands of a mob. For the violence of the crowd. For the many innocent who must suffer for the guilty.

WHAT AM I GOING TO DO ABOUT IT?

Resolutions: To remember the presence of God. Especially when I am tempted to sin. To remember that even though others are offending God, this does not give me a right to do it. That no matter what social ideals, or material gain, or modern mentality might have to say about morals and manners I must take my norms from Christ and His Church. To make an effort to alleviate the sufferings of the innocent.

PRAYER

Jesus Victim, I wish to comfort Thee; I unite myself to Thee, I offer myself in union with Thee; I count myself as nothing before Thee; I desire to forget myself in order to think of Thee, to be forgotten and despised for love of Thee; not to be understood, nor to be loved, except by Thee. I will hold my peace that I may listen to Thee. I will forsake myself that I may lose myself in Thee. Who livest and reigneth forever. Amen.

ASPIRATION

"Sacred Heart of Jesus, convert all poor blasphemers!" (*300 days' indul.; Racc. No. 241*).

The Hour of Rejection

THE prophet had seen in a vision the heartbreaking spectacle of the Passion of Christ. The one thing which shocked him was the malicious rejection of Christ by His own people. Shocked at what he saw, the prophet called upon inanimate nature to behold and be astonished at this rejection. "Be astonished at this, O ye heavens, and ye gates therefore be very desolate, saith the Lord. For my people have done two evils. They have forsaken me, the Fountain of Living Water, and have digged themselves cisterns – broken cisterns that can hold no water" (Jer. 2:12).

As the narrative of the Passion unfolds, the sufferings of Jesus, both of soul and body, increase in violence and intensity. In the rejection, Christ suffers in His soul, in His good name, in His honor, and in His dignity.

Our Blessed Lord was the promised Redeemer sent by God to restore to man the grace he had lost by original sin. This Redeemer had been described in great detail to the Jewish people by the inspired prophets. Two general characteristics had been specially emphasized. First, His suffering; and then, His glorious kingdom.

The people were material minded. If a man was well-to-do, they considered him pleasing to God. Thus, in time, the idea of a suffering Redeemer became lost. They looked forward to a conquering hero. But Isaias had recognized the Redeemer as . . . "despised and most abject of men, a man of sorrows and acquainted with infirmity" (Isa. 53:2).

Jesus certainly looked the part of the Man of Sorrows when the Sanhedrin handed Him over to Pilate as a conspirator. His Agony in the Garden, His betrayal and arrest, and His multiple mock trials had left their mark on Him.

Pilate, the pagan, feels sorry for our Lord and apparently presupposes the same sentiment in the people. He is rapidly and rudely disillusioned. Instead, they rejoice and gloat. In his effort to serve justice and save Christ from His enemies, Pilate tries what he thought was a smart bit of diplomacy. He sends for the worst villain in his dungeon – a man named Barabbas. This Barabbas was in prison for murder and sedition. He was the public enemy of that day. Pilate stands him next to Christ in the sight of the people.

Consider the shame of our Blessed Lord when He is rated as a criminal like Barabbas. What a sacrilegious insult to Him! The lawgiver is not distinguished from the lawbreaker. The author of life is bracketed with the destroyer of life. Pilate looks at the two. He passionately asks the howling mob: "Whom will you that I release unto you – Barabbas, or Jesus that is called the Christ?" (Mt. 27:17.) And St. Matthew tells us: "But the chief priests and ancients persuaded the people that they should ask for Barabbas, and make Jesus away" (Mt. 27:20). Pilate is stunned at this malicious choice. He

asks, "What shall I then do with Jesus that is called Christ?" (Mt. 27:22.) And St. Matthew tells us: "They cried out the more . . . Let him be crucified! Away with him" (Mt. 27:23).

So ends the story of the denial and rejection of Christ by those who should have known better. Jesus was not only compared to the worst kind of criminal but was actually judged to be worse than him. Jesus was not only rejected, but was condemned to die by His own people. The Sacred Heart of Christ is broken with shame and humiliation. In Him now is fulfilled the prophecy: "And with the wicked he was reputed" (Mk. 15:28).

The sad eyes of Christ look upon the frenzied mob who have just signed His death warrant. "His blood be upon us and upon our children" (Mt. 27:25).

The rejection of Christ was made by people who knew better. The rejection of Christ was made also by those who had benefited by His teaching, love, and miracles. Christ's heart was broken by this repulse. His love was officially spurned by those to whom He came first with redemption.

Why did Christ allow this rejection? The answer is simple. He wanted to teach us a lesson, one that cost Him dearly. It is this: Every man and woman has to make the choice between Christ and Barabbas, and it is not an easy choice. Barabbas was a criminal full of guilt and evil, a sinner grown glamorous with sin. He represents the world and everything contrary to Christ.

Our Blessed Lord stands for everything that is good and true and beautiful. Yet He is crushed and bruised and broken. If we follow the allurements of the world, we shall be its friends, its bosom companion. The world will love us and accept us as its own. If we choose to follow Christ, we shall be called upon to endure much for His sake and for the cause of religion. "For the disciple is not above the Master" (Lk. 6:40). It is not easy to live according to Christian faith and morality day after day. People are too soft. We must be constantly on guard lest we surrender. "For the Kingdom of Heaven suffereth violence, and only the violent bear it away" (Mt. 11:12).

If we choose to follow the despised Christ, our reward will be without measure. The Blessed Christ asked His disciples this leading question: "Ought not the Christ to have suffered all these things and thus enter into his glory?" (Lk. 24:26.) And St. Peter, speaking to the Jews on the rejection of Christ, gives us a wonderful promise of the reward for fidelity to Christ. "This Christ, the stone which was rejected by the builders, the same has become the head of the corner" (Acts 4:11). It is only by suffering and rejection that we can hope for heaven.

But if we weaken and prefer the world with its sins and pleasures, we reject Christ anew and cry out with the once chosen people of old: "Release unto us Barabbas" (Jn. 19:15). These are the words which broke the heart of Christ.

Jerusalem is no more. Why? Because that proud city and its arrogant inhabitants rejected Christ. "Jerusalem!" Our Blessed Lord called out as He wept over that vain city. "How often would I have gathered thee to my heart as a hen doth her brood, and thou wouldst not . . . " (Mt. 23:37).

Jesus Christ is the Man of the hour. Every hour is His triumph. He was rejected by a few and went on to save endless generations. When the hour of temptation comes to us, may we call down upon ourselves this blood which the Jews invoked. In our case, however, not with a will to murder, but with a thirst for the graces of redemption.

How to Meditate Further on This Chapter

COMPOSITION OF PLACE

a) *Physical:* The courtyard of Pilate, where his judgment seat is set up at the head of a long flight of stairs. The great crowd gathered about to see the end of Jesus. His enemies keeping their distance from such a pagan place lest they contact legal uncleanliness and be prevented from the observance of the great feast. The people of God turned against Him by their leaders. The messenger from Pilate's wife bidding her husband to have nothing to do with Jesus. The swaggering Barabbas. Jesus appareled as a mock king.

b) *Spiritual:* This is the hour of choice. Jesus had come unto His own, and in very truth they had "received him not." This was not so much the trial of Christ as the trial of the chosen people. Not so much a rejection of God as a rejection of God's people because they were too blind to see in Him the fulfillment of all prophecy. This was a bitter turning in the way. The point of no return. The choice to stand with . . . or against the God of Abraham, Isaac, and Jacob who, before any of these were, was the great "I am."

WHO IS IT THAT SUFFERS?

Here is the Creator who is rejected in favor of a creature. Here is the God of truth who is rejected in favor of a lie. Here is the Lawgiver who is rejected in favor of a lawbreaker. Here is the God of Life, who is made death that a sinner might go free. Here is He after whom all the hearts of men seek, and He is rejected in favor of a murderer and a seditionist.

WHAT DOES HE SUFFER?

a) *Spiritually:* This rejection of Jesus Christ is ultimately a sacrilege. The most consummate profanation of His holy person and His holy office. It is the rejection of every promise made by God to His people. The denial of every prophecy. The refusal to accept the redemption of God for the sins of men. Jesus then is made to suffer in His soul when He sees His work, His love, and His sufferings valued as nothing by the very ones He came *first* to save.

b) *Physically:* Behold Jesus Christ, clothed in mock purple, crowned with thorns, a broken reed in His hands, whip-lashed and blood-splashed, reputed with the wicked, indeed according to the testimony of Isaias . . . "despised and most abject of men, a man of sorrows and acquainted with infirmity" (Isa. 53:2). See His shame. See His confusion. See His sorrow and dereliction.

c) *Mentally:* Who indeed has known the mind of God? But how easy to essay the thoughts of the Son of Man. This was His own people who wanted no part of Him. These were the ones to whom He had come first. These were His first love. His first loyalty. His first choice. They willingly gave Him up. They chose another in His place. They were not sorry at this parting. They even called down His blood upon themselves and their children. In their false choice they broke the heart of their loving Redeemer, and closed the door against Him.

This is hard for Jesus to take. Worse than His physical pain is the pain in His heart that He is not wanted, not appreciated, not acceptable even to His own.

WHY DOES HE SUFFER?

a) *Chronologically:* Jesus suffers from the blindness of men. From the spiritual pride of a whole nation. From the envy out of which He had been delivered up. He suffers from being second choice. From the lack of love. The lack of gratitude. From being unknown and unrecognized. From shame. From humiliation.

b) *Mystically:* He suffers from my worldliness. From my choosing any person, or place, or thing in preference to Him. He suffers from my ingratitude. From my unmindfulness of His suffering for me. He suffers because I run away from suffering. Because I so often choose creatures instead of Him. My will over His. Because so often I overlook Him in the poor, the weak, the sick, the outcast, and seek my companionship with the glamorous, the wealthy, the powerful, the scandal givers, and the indifferent.

WHAT AM I GOING TO DO ABOUT IT?

Resolutions: I will always prefer God's will to my own. I will prefer rather to choose the crown of thorns with Him, than a crown of worldly renown. I will rejoice in His company and the company of those who love Him, rather than with the worldly, or those I can get something out of, or those who need not help nor companionship. In the thousand choices I have each day between Christ and Barabbas I will choose wisely and well. I will govern my life not by the question, How little can I do for my soul? but rather, How much more can I do to save my soul? I will atone for every neglect and rejection I have ever committed.

PRAYER

O God who, for the redemption of the world, didst will to be born among men, and by ancient rites admitted into the unity of Thy Chosen People, only to be rejected by them in the time of Thy Passion, grant to us who daily receive the merits of Thy redemption, that we may always stand with Thee, and choose only those things which please Thee, and that Thy Blood may be upon us not for a curse but for a blessing. Who livest and reignest forever. Amen.

ASPIRATION

"We therefore pray Thee help Thy servants, whom Thou hast redeemed with Thy Precious Blood" (*300 days' indul.; Racc. No. 215*).

The Hour of Condemnation

THE trials and imprisonment of Jesus were illegal according to Roman law. Under the treaty by which Palestine became a Roman province, the Jews could not inflict the death penalty without ratification from the Roman Governor. It now remained for Pontius Pilate, the military governor, to review the case of Jesus. Therefore, "Straightway in the morning the chief priests, holding a consultation with the ancients and scribes and the whole council, binding Jesus, led him away and delivered him to Pilate" (Mk. 15:1).

Pilate had set up his judgment seat in the courtyard of his palace. Court was usually held early so that officials could relax during the intense heat of midday. Pilate must have realized at once that something special was in the wind when he saw the multitude accompanying Jesus. All the principal men of Jerusalem were in the group.

Pilate was typical of a Roman official of that day. He was serving an apprenticeship in the country while awaiting promotion to some post in Rome. In a sense, he was on trial himself. The Jews had already reported him to Rome. They would do so again, finally provoking his removal and suicide. The Governor was haughty, contemptuous of this conquered people. Trained, however, in Roman justice, his sense of decency was aroused when he beheld the mistreatment of Jesus by the almost frenzied mob. Disdainfully he noticed how the people would not put a foot in his courtyard lest they defile themselves. It was hypocrisy like this that made Pilate fear and hate these Jews.

"Pilate therefore went out to them, and said to them: What accusation bring you against this man? They answered and said to him: If he were not a malefactor we would not have delivered him up to thee. Pilate therefore said to them: Take him you, and judge him according to your law" (Jn. 18:29).

This was the first round in the fight between Pilate and the Jews for a stake which was the life of Jesus. It was a thrust and a parry, a thrust by the Jews and a parry by Pilate. They were no further ahead than before, and Pilate was enjoying their discomfiture.

Fearing their case might not progress, the chief priests cried out from the gateway: "It is not lawful for us to put any man to death" (Jn. 18:31). This statement was true not only under the Roman treaty but even according to the Mosaic law, for a criminal could not be executed on the same day on which he was judged. But the ancients, wanting Jesus put out of the way at once, wanted a new trial for Him.

And they began to accuse Jesus, saying: "We have found this man perverting our nation, and forbidding to give tribute to Caesar, and saying that he is Christ, the King" (Lk. 23:2). As the Governor would understand these statements, they were lies. Looking at the

forlorn figure of Jesus, Pilate seizes another opportunity to revile the Jews and asks Christ if He is the King of the Jews.

"Jesus answered: Sayest thou this thing of thyself, or have others told it thee of me? Pilate answered: Am I a Jew? Thy own nation and chief priest have delivered thee up to me. What hast thou done?" (Jn. 18:33.)

To Pilate's astonishment, the weary and woebegone prisoner tells him that He has a kingdom which is not of this world. If it were of this world, His followers would have fought to prevent His falling into the hands of the Jews.

With amazement the Governor asks: "Art thou then a king? Jesus answered, thou sayest that I am a king. For this was I born and for this came I into the world; that I should give testimony of the truth. Everyone that is of the truth heareth my voice" (Jn. 18:37).

"And Pilate, calling together the chief priests and magistrates and the people, said to them: You have presented me this man, as one that perverteth the people. And behold I, having examined him before you, find no cause in this man, in those things wherein you accuse him. I will chastise him therefore and release him" (Lk. 23:13).

Here we see the folly of Pilate. Convinced of the innocence of Jesus, he tries to appease the Jews. If they wish Jesus punished, the Governor will do so, not by imposing the death penalty, but by ordering a sound beating. But obviously this is not enough. Nothing but death will satisfy the mob.

Pilate weakly tries again, offering a second choice. Which of the two would they like him to release, Jesus or the infamous Barabbas? Like many another politician, before and since, Pilate is caught in his own trap. The people call for the release of Barabbas and the death of Jesus.

Pilate is stunned.

"He said to them the third time. Why, what evil hath this man done? I find no cause of death in him. I will chastise him and let him go.

"But they were insistent with loud voices requiring that he might be crucified. And their voices prevailed.

"And Pilate gave sentence that it should be as they required" (Lk. 23:22).

And what was their loud-voiced insistence about? "We have no king but Caesar" (Jn. 19:15). "If thou release this man, thou art not Caesar's friend. For whosoever maketh himself a king speaketh against Caesar" (Jn. 19:12).

So, though he knew Jesus was an innocent victim of hatred, and though he had had a mysterious message from his wife who had suffered much in a dream because of Jesus, Pilate condemned Jesus to death.

"Pilate seeing that he prevailed nothing, but that rather a tumult was made, taking water washed his hands before the people, saying: I am innocent of the blood of this just man. Look you to it. And the whole people answering, said: his blood be upon us and upon our children" (Mt. 27:24).

This is the story of the condemnation of Jesus – a manifold display of malice, appeasement, and gross instability.

Malice on the part of the leaders of the Jews, who could have easily recognized Jesus as the Messias had they not been envious of His influence over the people, jealous of their own position and acquired rights, and blind to the manifest works of God under their eyes.

Appeasement on the part of Pilate, who feared the Jews as much as he hated them. The Governor punished innocence with slaughter, so that his position might be secure with Caesar.

Instability on the part of the people. With almost miraculous caprice, they strewed palm and sang Hosannas on Sunday, and on Friday they cried out "Crucify him!" "His blood be upon us, and upon our children."

Jesus Christ is the Man of the Hour. Every hour is His triumph. In this hour He overcomes His enemies by using their malice to bring about God's will that He should die upon the cross for love of us. In this hour, He overcomes the political intrigue and lack of principle in Pilate by boldly declaring that this is the reason why He came into the world, to die for principle and for truth — the principle and the truth being that God so loved the world that He even gave His only Son as a sacrifice for us. And finally in this hour, Jesus triumphs over the fickleness of the people by showing His great love for them in willingly accepting His condemnation and offering His precious blood for them.

But the hour of the condemnation of Christ is not over. Daily, evil makes friends with evil at the expense of Christ. Nation with nation and individual with individual. Politicians still trade Christ for their own positions. Warmakers and warmongers condemn the innocent to death and deliver them up out of envy. The lesson from the condemnation of Christ is this: A man can have no real power over others if he does not first have it over himself. Truth is objective, and virtue is its own reward. A reign of injustice and appeasement is a recipe for nothing but chaos.

The miniaturists, whose illustrations decorate the pages of the medieval Hour Books, portray Pilate in a state of collapse, sprawled in his curule chair, with a towel hanging from his hand, the picture of dejection and frustration. Here is the man who had the chance to make history but who loved himself more than justice, more than truth, and more than God. In this generation of frustrated souls, salvation lies with Christ who called His disciples together and said:

"You know that the princes of the gentiles lord it over them, and they that are the greater exercise power upon you. . . . It shall not be so among you. . . . And he that will be first among you shall be your servant. Even as the Son of Man is not come to be ministered unto, but to minister and give his life a redemption for many" (Mt. 20:25).

How to Meditate Further on This Chapter

COMPOSITION OF PLACE

a) *Physical:* This scene occurs in Pilate's place of judgment. His official chair of judgment has been placed on the platform at the head of what is called today the "Holy Stairs." Jesus stands before him, purpling these steps with His most Precious Blood. The people have rejected their king. Pilate has declared Christ innocent yet has condemned Him to be scourged. And this is not enough. Now the crowd will have the death of Jesus. And Pilate forgets the law. He forgets justice. He lampoons judgment. And out of craven fear he appeases those who have delivered up Jesus Christ out of envy and issues the death sentence against the Saviour of the world.

b) Spiritual: In spirit look upon Jesus the innocent Lamb of God. This is His triumph even though it appears to be His defeat. Now when no one wants Him, when He is rejected, mocked, and despised, He declares Himself a King. He accepts the judgment against Himself, saying. "For this was I born, and for this came I into the world, to give testimony of the truth." And Pilate gives Jesus one last humiliation asking, "What is truth?" Pilate adds insult to injury by belittling this Man-God who is Truth itself.

WHO IS IT THAT SUFFERS?

This is none other than He who is without sin. He dared His enemies to find any sin in Him and they could not. He is the Lamb of God who takes away the sins of the world. He is the way, the truth, and the life. He is our Judge who is condemned. He is our Life who is made death for us. And He is the Lover of souls who is willing to die that we may have life and have it more abundantly.

WHAT DOES HE SUFFER?

a) Spiritually: In His holy soul Jesus Christ suffers from outraged justice. He suffers from the denial of the truth. From the abuse of laws both of God and man. He suffers from the imminence of His cruel death. He suffers the horror that the Innocent must always endure when they are accused unjustly.

b) Physically: Jesus Christ now suffers the worst indignity possible for a man. He is to endure the supreme penalty of the death of the body. And this for crimes of which He is guiltless. He is condemned. Yet the guilty are His judges and His jury. He is to die for the sins of others. Yet He Himself is without stain. His judge washes his hands in an empty gesture, as if he is not to blame for what he has done knowingly and willingly. Yet no amount of washing can ever blot out the ignominy of the condemnation of the Innocent Christ by the guilt of those who should have known better.

c) *Mentally:* We who are so lacking in justice, so lacking in judgment, and so lacking in prudence, cannot understand the pain Jesus endured in this phase of His Passion. Christ knew better than all, the law, the motives, and the malice that were stacked up against Him in this hour. He Himself would judge the world . . . but the world had a chance, for His justice would be tempered with mercy. Yet here the world judges Him and justice is beclouded by malice and envy and jealousy and selfishness.

WHY DOES HE SUFFER?

a) *Chronologically:* Jesus suffers in His reputation, being condemned as a malefactor. Yet He suffers willingly because He has come into the world in order to show man God's great love for him. The proof of His love will be His death on the cross. He desires the cross. But the manner of His condemnation is a further humiliation for the Blessed Christ. This He endures for the love of us.

b) *Mystically:* He suffers for me and for my lack of judgment. He suffers for my rash judgment of others. For my interpreting their actions in the light of my own weakness. He suffers for all those who are unjustly condemned. He suffers for all the false trials of the ages. He suffers for the condemnation of His saints. For the lies and false witness brought against His Church. For the heresies and schisms to come. And for all those who deny the truth. He suffers because of the condemnation I deserve for my sins.

WHAT AM I GOING TO DO ABOUT IT?

Resolutions: I will try to live up to the virtue of justice in my life. To render to God what is His due . . . my adoration, my sorrow for sin, my thanksgiving, and my petitions for the graces I need. I will render to my neighbor all that belongs to him . . . by defending his good name, by respecting his property and his right to it, and by honoring his rights as well as my own. I will even remember my rights and duties toward myself by striving to be honest with myself, and avoiding the occasions of sin.

PRAYER

O my Jesus, I should stand condemned forever because of my many sins, yet I see Thee condemned to death by an unjust judgment. By Thy sufferings in that hour, spare me from the condemnation that is to come, and be merciful unto me a sinner. Who livest and reignest forever. Amen.

ASPIRATION

"St. Michael the Archangel, defend us in the battle, that we may not perish in the fearful judgment" (*300 days' indul.; Racc. No. 442*).

The Hour of Reparation

JESUS CHRIST is the Man of the Hour, and every hour is His triumph. In this hour we shall consider the scourging of our Blessed Lord at the pillar, when Christ suffered in a special manner for the selfishness of men.

The superabundant sufferings of the Passion will always remain a tremendous mystery. Christ our Saviour is the all-holy and sinless One made like unto us in all things, sin only excepted. Upon Him, however, was laid the burden of our sins. "He was wounded for our iniquities: he was bruised for our sins" (Isa. 53:5). There is an inexorable law of divine retribution laid down by the Holy Ghost in the Book of Wisdom: "By what things a man sinneth, by the same also is he tormented" (Wisd. 11:17). This, then, is the key to an initial understanding of the scourging of Christ. Willingly taking our sins upon Himself, He suffers in His innocent flesh for us.

The Gospel is terse in its narration of the scourging. The scene is related in a single sentence. The Apostles and Evangelists, so close even in time to the reality of this shocking scene, are reticent about details, because of the horror it gave them and the depth of their personal love for Jesus.

The scene must have progressed in this wise. Our Blessed Lord was led off to the place of the scourging. Every criminal was scourged before crucifixion, but at this time Pilate had no intention of crucifying Christ. He was manifestly going to scourge Him and let Him go. Therefore this was to be a special kind of scourging, a Roman punishment reserved for rebellious slaves. The Jewish scourging was forty strokes less one, so that the victim would not die under the lash. The Roman scourging before crucifixion was also limited, at least by a vicious prudence, lest the victim not live to be crucified.

But, as our Lord is stripped and tied to the pillar, His tormentors have no law to limit their fury. Here is a man come to them in a fool's garment – one who claimed to be king, so the people said. These soldiers would teach Him what it meant to rebel against the yoke of Rome. Jesus is stripped of His garments, His hands tied above His head to the column of flagellation. The soldiers appointed for the scourging take their place on each side of Jesus, holding the leather thongs tipped with lead or bone which the Roman custom warranted in such a case. They are rough and ribald men, hardened to immunity concerning the feelings of others.

Consider the difference between them and our Blessed Lord. Here is the most beautiful of the sons of men. He of the healing hands. He of the noble face, the lordly bearing. He of the sensitive and delicate body, which serves only to hide His very divinity. What shame and embarrassment for Him as He stands stripped of His garments, with His sacred body laid bare, waiting for the lash. A spectacle to all eyes!

B BRAMANTI

With experienced and muscular strokes the soldiers begin their work. One stroke follows upon another with maddening regularity. Each stroke leaves its mark – a blue welt on the body of Christ. Repeated blows send crimson rivulets running to the ground. How long this unmerciful beating lasted we do not know. Perhaps until the soldiers themselves were exhausted. Certainly the sufferings of Christ were not considered.

Historians of the time, such as Josephus, Tacitus, and Cicero, use vigorous language to describe a scourging. The lashes, they tell us . . . "bite" . . . "tear" . . . and "furrow" the flesh. Cicero records a scourging that did not stop until a man's bones were laid bare. And the gentle Christ was treated no better than any other criminal.

The scourging over, the ropes or chains holding the body of the victim were loosened. The whip-lashed and blood-splashed Christ collapsed onto the pavement, reddened and warmed with His own precious blood. How can we bear to look longer at our gentle Saviour so much abused.

Well did the Prophet Isaias write of Him: "From the crown of his head to the sole of his foot: There is no soundness in him" (Isa. 1:6). The Prophet David, seeing the Messias in this utterly reduced condition, puts these words of the psalms in the mouth of Christ, "I am a worm and no man!" (Ps. 21:7.) And, on Good Friday, holy Mother Church sings with a plaintive eloquence, in the name of Christ at the pillar . . . "My people, my people! What have I done to thee? Answer me. Thou hast scourged me, and delivered me up."

Why did Christ suffer so? Why did the God-Man lay bare His virginal flesh to the lashes? Why does Christ, the sinless One, lay in a crumpled heap at the foot of a blood-stained pillar? Why? Because of sin! Christ is reduced to this shameful state to atone for every offense man has or will commit against God. "The chastisement of our peace is upon him . . . and by his bruises we are healed" (Isa. 53:5). Christ is suffering in our stead. The Fathers of the Church tell us that Christ suffered the scourging in a special manner for those sins of men which defile the body.

Of all the sins by which man defiles his body, the chief is the sin of impurity, so rampant in our day. Sins of the married. Sins of the single. Sins committed together. Sins committed alone. Sins that make men and women lower than beasts. These are the sins that brought Christ down in a crumpled heap at the column of the flagellation, bathed in sweat and tears and blood.

Today impurity is taken for granted. It is not even considered bad taste. At most it is considered a human weakness — an easy way out. Some polluted minds in education and medicine urge unrestrained sex pleasure for the unmarried as necessary compensation. What madness to think so little of so great an evil!

Would you know the malice of the sin of impurity? Look at it not as the world does, but as God does. The sin of impurity at the time of Noe made God repent that He had ever made man! The sin of impurity in the time of Lot caused God to rain down fire and brimstone on the cities of the plain, the ill-odored and ill-fated Sodom and Gomorrah.

The sin of impurity has always brought with it its own punishment both for body and soul. Nervous frustration and mental debility are the crown of its devotees.

Everywhere today, this sin is condoned and applauded

— in newspapers, books, shows, magazines, and even over the radio and television. There is only one place where one can see this sin in its true light. Only one place where God's evaluation of impurity can be seen. In the blood-stained, crumpled figure of the God-Man, who looks with tear-filled eyes from the place where He has fallen, beaten and bruised and broken, for love of men.

St. Thomas Aquinas tells us that upon the capital vice of lust and impurity there follow these daughter evils: blindness of mind, rashness, unmindfulness, inconstancy, self-love, hatred of God, cleaving to the present life, and horror of the world to come. He points out that all these have one thing in common, that the mind is absorbed by the flesh. One might think the Angelic Doctor had been reading the modern daily press. Self-love pervades the hearts of men and women today as never before.

The effects of our present-day belittling of holy purity have brought forth a generation blind to the sufferings of Christ and the law of God. Our youth is rash beyond belief, willing to take any chance in time or eternity for thrills of the flesh. People are no longer constant in their efforts to avoid occasions of sin. God is hated in many parts of the world because He tells us as our Creator that we do not have sole dominion over our bodies. The attitude of this generation is to live for the moment. Heaven has nothing to offer to the children of this world, who find satisfaction only in their own selfishness and its satisfaction in their own flesh.

We may indeed be amused by the grotesque and exaggerated hideousness of the daughters of lust as they gloat over the scourged Christ in medieval illustrated Passion meditations, but their artistic excess is far nearer to pleasing God than the sophisticated indifference of today's children to the Christ of the Pillar and their lost sense of sin.

The scourging of Christ is an object lesson to the modern world. The lesson is clear. Selfishness begets sins of the flesh. And Christ's triumph in this hour is to show men that their sins will not go unpunished.

How to Meditate Further on This Chapter

COMPOSITION OF PLACE

a) Physical: This scene in the Passion of Jesus took place in the great stone courtyard of the barracks. Here Jesus is stripped of His garments. His hands are fastened high above His head thus stretching out His body to receive the maximum impact of the scourges. His tormentors spare neither Him nor themselves. The hard tipped leather thongs swing in deadly monotony. The pure body of Jesus shows the welts. Then the bruises. Then the open wounds of torn flesh. For the second time in the Passion the earth runs red with the saving flood of the precious blood.

b) Spiritual: This particularly violent mystery of the sacred Passion is also the object lesson of divine retribution. Every man will suffer in those things in which he offends God. The wealthy lose their earthly goods. The proud are brought down in weakness and senility. The devotees of the flesh suffer in their bodies, for no sin more surely leaves its traces than lust. But Jesus who is without sin, is made sin for us. He suffers in our stead. It is precisely this torment of the body, the shame of exposure and the pain of His more sensitive body that makes this suffering of Jesus an act of reparation for the sins of the flesh.

WHO IS IT THAT SUFFERS?

Behold the Son of God and the Son of the Blessed Virgin Mary. See Him who was once the most beautiful of the sons of men disfigured from head to foot. See the Innocent suffer for the guilty. The most perfect body to come forth from the hand of God and the flesh of woman, most cruelly tormented.

WHAT DOES HE SUFFER?

a) *Spiritually:* In this mystery of the scourging of Jesus we see God suffering for the sins of men. He has taken upon Himself a body. He has become like unto us in all things with the exception of sin. But now He clothes Himself not only with humanity but in a reparative sense with one of the most common of the sins of humanity and covers Himself with its punishments. How the soul of Jesus hated sin. How He suffered because of it. How much did He adore the will of the Father, and therefore how humbly did He accept this exposure of body and torment of flesh to atone for all sins, but even more especially for the sins of the body.

b) *Physically:* The very delicacy of the body of Christ is physically one of the principal causes of His pain in the scourging. Now when the blessed body of Jesus is described as delicate it does not mean that He was weak or sickly. It means that He was so perfect in form and physique that His perceptions were more intense, His reflexes more perfect, and His senses more acute, than those of ours which are dulled by sin and debilitated by physical imperfections. Therefore physically the scourging was more painful to Jesus than it would have been to us. The lashes . . . the welts . . . the torn flesh . . . the biting wounds . . . all stung Jesus with a nicety we can never appreciate. This then is the consummate mystery of the Passion. The willingness of Jesus to suffer. The exceptional ability to feel suffering. And the superabundance of suffering He endured.

c) *Mentally:* This stage of the Passion afflicts the gentle Jesus not only from without but also from within. He sees the multiple sins of the flesh for which He is tormented. His modesty is chagrined by the exposure of His holy body to the gaze of the sinful and ribald soldiery. He is made indeed a spectacle before angels and men. Even in His pain He has no privacy. Yet neither does He have compassionate companions. He is surrounded by His enemies and His tormentors. He is alone again.

WHY DOES HE SUFFER?

a) *Chronologically:* Jesus Christ suffers in time because of the weakness of Pilate trying to appease the people at His expense. He suffers from the lashes of the scourges. From the cords or chains that bind His hands. He suffers from the joy of the people who gloat over His misery. He suffers in a special way to atone for all the sins of men but especially for every sin of the flesh and every selfish act of mankind.

b) *Mystically:* From all by intemperance in eating and drinking Jesus suffers. From every preference of myself to Him or to His commandments. From the sins of impurity found at such an alarmingly young age and at such a disappointingly old age in our generation, and at all the stages in between. From the sins of youth. From the sins of the unmarried. From the sins of the married who turn a holy state into an occasion of sin for each other. From the immodesty of dress everywhere so common. From the ribald story and the obscene joke. From the wantonness of the stage and screen. Jesus falls to the ground after His scourging but He has been covered with the slime of man's earthiness from the very first stroke of the lash.

WHAT AM I GOING TO DO ABOUT IT?

Resolutions: I will endeavor to keep my body pure and my soul holy. I will be careful of my eyes. Of what I read. Of what I see. I will guard my thoughts lest I add fuel to the concupiscence of my flesh. I will avoid dangerous amusements. I will shun the company of those who tell and listen to smutty stories. I will avoid every companion who leads me into sin, remembering that it is better to have twelve enemies than one friend who may lead me into sin. I will mortify my flesh that in time of temptation I will be able to overcome it.

PRAYER

O God, who for our salvation willed in the taking up of our mortal flesh to be scourged at the pillar, mercifully grant that we, who recall to mind the memory of this sacred mystery, may merit to share forever in the fruit of Thy most precious blood. Who livest and reignest forever. Amen.

ASPIRATION

"O good Jesus, within Thy wounds hide me" (*300 days' indul.; Racc. No. 199*).

The Hour of Mockery

THE head is the most noble member of the human body. Physically, because here sense perceptions are processed into material for intellectual knowledge. Mentally, because the human brain governs, from the head, all the other members of the body. And spiritually, because here reside the intentions and aspirations of human nature, the first operations of the intellectual soul of man, distinguishing between good and evil, choosing the good, the true, and the beautiful. The ancients honored art and poetry and writing by crowning the head with laurel. Even athletes received a crown for the exercise of the body. Kings were given crowns to signify their wisdom and the dignity of their office. It is precisely because of its nobility that the human head is honored.

Even nature gives a special protection to the head. In imminent danger, at an accident, the first impulse is to protect the head. It is precisely the honorable position of the head that makes the abuse of it so insulting and revolting. The emissaries of the ancient Hebrews were contumeliously treated by having half their heads shaved.

A blow in the face is the highest affront, an invitation to a duel to death. The Passion of Jesus is referred to by the sacred liturgy as the "duel between life and death." Therefore we should not be surprised to see in the history of the Passion of Jesus the most insulting abuse heaped on the sacred head of Jesus.

The mistreatment of the head of Christ reached its climax in the second mocking of Jesus. He had already been reviled by the Jews during His all-night imprisonment, and now He was assailed by the Roman soldiers. Indeed, they gathered together the whole band, about five hundred men, to witness the shameful treatment of Jesus.

The evangelist describes this scene for us, "Then the soldiers of the Governor, taking Jesus in the hall, gathered together unto him the whole band, and stripping him they clothed him with purple. And platting a crown of thorns, they put it upon his head, and a reed in his right hand. And bowing the knee before him, they began to salute him, and they mocked him, saying: 'Hail king of the Jews.' And spitting upon him, they took the reed and struck his head" (Mt. 27:27).

The scourging of Jesus was hardly over when this new suffering began. The whole cohort was assembled to watch this sport of a mock King. An old military cloak, long discarded, was thrown about the bruised and bleeding shoulders of Christ. His holy hands, still bound from the ring of the pillar of flagellation, received a broken reed for a scepter. A crown only was wanting to Jesus Christ the King. Satan himself seems to have been the designer of the diadem of thorns. The soldiers discovered at hand the twining branches of the briar, covered with sharp points within and without. From this was the

B·BRAMANTI

crown of Jesus made, amid coarse jests and curses, when the soldiers' hands were pricked by the spikes.

From the testimony of holy visionaries and the actual relic of the crown of thorns, carried by St. Louis, ninth of the name to rule France, and placed in the rare architectural gem called the Sainte Chapelle in Paris, the crown was actually a cap, with thorns woven over and across the head. This was a wreath with cross strands. Thus, when Jesus was crowned, the whole crown of His head was pierced with thorns. So difficult was this instrument of torture for the soldiers to handle that it was necessary to push it down and force it into place by the use of rods, this being the reason for the soldiers' striking Jesus on the head.

It is almost impossible to imagine the intensity of pain which the crowning with thorns caused the sacred head and humanity of the God-Man. St. Leonard of Port Maurice, the fiery Franciscan preacher of the eighteenth century, gives this testimony: "A single thorn that penetrates the foot of a lion causes him so much pain that the King of the Beasts roars and rages and fills the forest with his howling. What a terrible pain, then, must so many thorns have caused, which penetrated not the padded foot, but the tender head of Jesus. Indeed, when the head suffers the pain cannot be slight; and what would only be a slight pain in any other member of the body becomes in the head a veritable torture."

All the time Jesus has in this world from now until His death, He will bear the crown of thorns. Even when they once more dress Him in His own clothes, the diadem of throbbing pain is left upon His brow. And the reason for this is the shocking realization that it could not be removed without directly causing the death of Christ, so deeply is it embedded in His matted scalp.

While the head of Jesus is racked with this pain, the soldiers, admiring their costuming and make-up of the mock king, salute Him with the most vile insults. This time, the eyes of Jesus are not veiled, and He sees His tormentors with their leering smiles and mock genuflections. On Good Friday, the Church puts this reproach into the mouth of the suffering Saviour: "My people, My people, what have I done to thee? Or in what have I saddened thee? To thee I gave a royal scepter, and thou hast given My head a crown of thorns. For thee I have slain the kings of Canaan, and thou hast beaten My head with a reed."

The astounding element of all the scenes of the Passion of Jesus is His silence. Never does He complain. Never does He cry out. Not even at this hateful demonstration.

The medieval artists, whose souls were so full of faith, have a happy faculty of knowing the essentials in the Passion. Their penchant for illustration of the mocking of Christ accentuates beyond measure the crowning with thorns. They try to illustrate the number of thorns by winding almost ridiculous lengths of thorns about the head of Jesus. They knew that Christ was a King. He was willing to suffer this indignity because He is a King of Sorrows. And this He is by His free choice. In the act of man crowning Jesus with sharp thorns, the artist of the Middle Ages saw a mystical triumph of the silent Christ, receiving a crown after His own heart.

Jesus Christ is indeed the Man of the Hour. Every hour of time sees His triumph. As the King of loving hearts, His painful crowning as a mock king is a great victory. Since that day, many a royal crown has been discarded for the thorny crown of Christ. Many a youthful heart has been moved to prefer a hidden life in the cloister to a crown of worldly success. The thorn-crowned King still triumphs.

The holy Fathers and Doctors of the Church point out that, despite the good effects in latter days of the crowning of Jesus, the same evil causes that produced it still exist. It is the almost universal opinion of those who write on the crowning with thorns that Jesus endured this suffering in a special way to atone for sins of thought. In a world so indifferent to the law of God, our present Holy Father has declared that the greatest sin of humanity today is its loss of the sense of sin. From Sinai, God thundered the last two commandments, which are directed specifically against sins of the mind. This generation needs to be reminded of the reality and iniquity of sins of the mind. There are among the damned in hell souls that were never guilty of any evil or impure action but who nevertheless were found hateful to God because of grievous sins of thought.

The sins of thought fall into three modes: Morose delectation or a morbid delight in beholding someone else's sin or in contemplating the commission of such a sin ourselves. Joy with which we are again enjoying the pleasure attached to already committed sins. And lastly, desire, which is a craving for sin that is consented to by the mind. As can at once be seen, any one of these modes can be ascribed to any kind of sin. Thus sins of thought, no matter what their mode, can be committed not only against purity, but also against justice and charity, faith and hope, temperance and prudence. And to see how displeasing to God are these sins of thought, one need only call to mind the Sacred Head of Christ crowned with thorns.

How wicked are those who compose or produce books, stage plays, and motion pictures which are calculated to arouse passion and evil thoughts in their spectators! What shall we say of those responsible for the sale of pornographic periodicals to our teen-agers of the corner-store variety? In the light of the crowning with thorns, who can whitewash those who make their livelihood on calumny and detraction – whose whole purpose is to make money by sowing discord, suspicion, and rash judgments in the minds of their readers? And are the avid readers of the above less worthy of censure? Let us listen to the scathing condemnation of Christ, the thorn-crowned King:

"Let them alone. They are blind leaders of the blind" (Mt. 15:14). "For from the heart come forth evil thoughts, murders, adulteries, fornications, thefts, false testimonies, blasphemies. These are the things that defile a man" (Mt. 15:19).

How to Meditate Further on This Chapter

COMPOSITION OF PLACE

a) *Physical:* The guardroom in the Praetorium. The band of Roman soldiers gathered about Jesus Christ. He has been beaten within an inch of His life. His holy body reduced to shreds. Now He is clothed with mock purple. A broken reed is placed in His hand to show forth the weakness of this King and the pretensions of His kingdom. And last of all He is crowned with thorns as a mockery of His kingship.

b) *Spiritual:* In this mystery of the Passion of Jesus He is made to suffer greatly in His office as King. Jesus

Christ is a King, having inherited His kingdom and royalty according to the flesh through King David, His noble ancestor. Jesus Christ is King because He is the head and the first-born of all creation. This fact is now ridiculed. This holy office mocked. This great dignity assailed by the ribald jests of sinful men.

WHO IS IT THAT SUFFERS?

This is Jesus Christ. The King of Ages, immortal and invisible, to whom honor and praise are ever due. This is He whose kingdom is not of this world. Whose kingdom has no end. Whose rule is forever. And whom to serve is to reign.

WHAT DOES HE SUFFER?

a) *Spiritually:* Christ the King suffers in His soul as He is mocked by men. He suffers as He is made the fool. He suffers because He is a King. He suffers as His office is belittled. He is a King and a Prophet. Yet His enemies cry out, "Prophesy unto us who it was that struck thee!" He is a true king, the very King of kings, and yet His kingship is ridiculed. "Hail, King!" And this from an unbelieving heart and sneering lips.

b) *Physically:* Jesus Christ suffers from the cords which bind His holy hands so tightly. An aggravation that is increased by the swelling caused by the welts of the scourges. His bleeding back is irritated by the roughness of the filthy mantle swung over His shoulders. His holy head is pierced again and again by the sharp thorns that cover His entire head and even push down on the nape of His neck. His eyes are dimmed by the constant flow of blood. Every movement is an agony. Every motion a pain to be shunned. Tension rises in His holy body. His blessed head aches and throbs and dizziness adds to His great discomfort. His head becomes a burden too painful to support. Too sore to be laid down. Too heavy to be held up, with its fierce encompassing of thorns.

c) *Mentally:* The indignity of human malice reaches its climax in the insults offered to the holy head of Jesus Christ. His shame is increased by the number who behold His humiliation. His modesty is outraged. His dignity forgotten. His person despised. His office denied. His rights rejected. His reputation reduced to naught. Not one moment of privacy is left to Him. Not one bit of solace. He is truly poured out as wax . . . unable to resist, unwilling to defend Himself, and covered with the uncontrollable hatred of men who make sport of His every misery.

WHY DOES HE SUFFER?

a) *Chronologically:* Jesus Christ the King suffers to atone for the sins of men. Especially for sins of pride and arrogance. For sins of angry and rebellious thoughts. For sins of impurity of mind. He suffers because He is a King whose kingdom is rather the hearts of men than the powers of earth. He suffers because all hell is out to prevent the establishment of His kingdom. Those who would have no king but Caesar repudiate this King of Hearts.

b) *Mystically:* I can see in the bound hands of Christ the liberty allowed my own. In His broken scepter the number of times I have broken His law. In His thorn crowned head all my proud, vain, jealous, envious, slothful, angry, violent, impure, and unfaithful thoughts. I can see in the mockery of His kingship my own stubborn will resisting His rule in my heart. I can hear in the cries of His enemies the cries of my own sins which exclaim with Satan of old, "I will not serve."

WHAT AM I GOING TO DO ABOUT IT?

Resolutions: I will see Christ as my King. He has conquered my heart by the depths of His humiliation for me. He has purchased me by His blood. He has won me as the prize of His battle against sin, death, and hell. For this then I will try and be His good servant. I will watch over my thoughts. I will guard my mind against the assaults of the world, the flesh, and the devil. I will be careful of what I read. Of what I look at. Of the entertainment I seek. I will remember how much Jesus has forgiven me and I will try to forgive others quickly and to forget my humiliations readily.

PRAYER

Grant, we beseech Thee, O almighty God, that as we venerate the crown of thorns of our Lord Jesus Christ the King, meditating on His Passion on earth, we may be made worthy to share His crown with Him forever in heaven. Who livest and reignest forever. Amen.

ASPIRATION

"Jesus, King and Center of all Hearts, by the coming of Thy Kingdom, grant us peace" (*300 days' indul.; Racc. No. 268*).

The Hour of Opportunity

OUR meditations on the Passion draw near to the climax of the sufferings of Christ, when, at this eleventh hour, we recall the carrying of the cross. In the beautifully illustrated medieval Hour Books, the carrying of the cross is usually portrayed as a triumphal march for Christ. And so it is. Jesus Christ is truly the victor, and every hour sees His victory over sin and the devil. Although the miniaturists of the Middle Ages represented the people along the way of the cross with a violence of expression and gesture, they idealized Christ. Like modern counterparts of the Beuronese school, their Christ walks erect and aloof from the taunting of His enemies. It is the last phase of His long-awaited Passion.

The eleventh hour has a specific connotation for us moderns of a kind of wonderful opportunity, a last-minute success story. A time of jubilant relief is the eleventh hour when, at the last minute, hopes are revived, confidence is restored, and ultimate victory is assured.

And such was the hour when Christ began the carrying of the cross. It was His wonderful opportunity. In this hour were the hopes of the men of all times revived. In this dread hour was their confidence in the mercy of God expanded beyond understanding.

The cross is the focal point of history. It is the only thing in which we Christians ought to glory, according to St. Paul, and it is the price of our salvation. The cross overshadowed the life of Christ and it overshadows the life of every Christian. "If any one wishes to come after me, let him . . . take up his cross and follow me" (Mt. 16:24).

Pilate had three times declared Jesus innocent; now he orders Him to be crucified. Our divine Lord has longed for this moment. "I have a baptism with which I am to be baptized, and how I am straitened until it be accomplished" (Lk. 12:50). The Jews too have waited for this moment, for they said: "It is expedient that one man should die, rather than the whole nation perish" (Jn. 11:50).

It was ordained by Roman Law that the condemned carry his own cross. Christ was to be no exception to the law.

Our Blessed Lord is again clothed in His own garments. This is done that the people may recognize Him. With a wicked cunning, the crown of thorns is deliberately left on the head of Christ. The procession to the place of execution is begun. First go the soldiers, who break a way in the narrow streets crowded with the noonday throngs. Then comes a herald announcing the crimes of the condemned. After follow the thieves and the rest of the guards. Our Blessed Lord is the central figure of this motley group. He is indeed a pitiful spectacle. How rough and painful is this journey for Him! Jesus has been without food or drink since the Last Supper. His

shoulders and back are so torn and wounded by the scourging that even the weight of His clothes is an agony, yet now He bears the full weight of the heavy wood of the cross. As if this were not enough, Christ is goaded on by His executioners and jostled and mocked by the crowd. His every movement is a shock of pain, and his blood-stained footprints mark out the way to Calvary forever.

What are the interior thoughts in Christ's Sacred Heart as He is led as a lamb to the slaughter? He looks about Him at the milling crowd. These are the very ones who four days ago strewed palms in His way and cried out: "Blessed is he that cometh . . . Hosanna" (Mt. 21:9). Now they curse Him. Here He sees one to whom He restored the gift of speech, and that man is calling out for His precious blood. Again He sees one to whom He gave sight, but a cruel, pitiless hate gleams in those eyes cured by a loving glance of the Saviour.

Jesus Christ is broken in body and in heart. He looks toward Calvary. His strength is exhausted. He falls! The sacred face of Christ is buried in the dust of the street. Jesus rises under a rain of blows and kicks, only to struggle till He falls again. While the Stations of the Cross honor only three falls, these represent many other falls brought about by the exhausted condition of our Saviour.

The enemies of Christ are getting anxious. What if He should die before He reaches Calvary? Word is sent to the centurion that he should get someone to help Jesus and save their criminal for death on the cross. When it becomes known that the soldiers are looking for a helper to bear the cross, the crowd shies away. No Roman would carry the cross; it was the vilest form of execution. No Roman citizen could be executed on a cross, so why should they help another? No Jew would touch the cross, for it was written plainly in the law, "Cursed is he that hangeth upon the tree" (Deut. 21:23).

No one to be had? The eyes of Christ search the faces of the crowd. A Hebrew from Cyrene is seen by the soldiers. He is stopped and ordered to help with the cross. He has no choice. Who can resist the Roman empire? Better to walk in disgrace in a strange city than suffer a worse fate for resistance. Simon begrudgingly takes up the cross of Christ, and both head for Calvary. He finds his disgrace is in reality a grace. Christ and Simon bear the cross as beasts bear the yoke. It is not long until Simon realizes that the yoke of Christ is sweet and His burden is light.

We have here a great mystery. We know that our divine Lord was God. He could have had angels bear His cross for Him. He could have relieved Himself of this burden by His own miraculous powers. But He deliberately allowed Himself to suffer the cross so keenly that He almost expired. He wanted someone to help Him. When all bystanders refused, He gave this grace to a stranger. Why did Christ let a man help? Because He wanted to teach us all a lesson. What is the lesson? Christ shared His cross with a man and gave that man the grace to suffer gladly and the greater grace to save his soul, to show us the necessity of salvation through the cross.

This is a most vital and important lesson: that the cross by which we are redeemed is to be borne, not by Christ alone, but by every one of His followers. All of Divine Revelation clearly teaches us that God will not save us without our co-operation. If we are then to cooperate in our salvation, if we are to save our immortal souls, we must use the same means God has chosen to effect our redemption, namely, the cross.

How, then, are we to save ourselves by the cross? St. Augustine gives us an excellent example. He tells us that three men carried crosses to Calvary and three men died on their crosses that fateful day. Christ carried His cross and died upon it with perfect resignation to the will of His heavenly Father — and so the cross of Christ became the redemption of the world. One thief carried his cross and died thereon in a spirit of humility and patience. He confessed his sins and acknowledged the justice of his punishment. The cross became for him the tree of Life, for he had the happiness of hearing Christ Himself tell him: "This day thou shalt be with me in paradise" (Lk. 22:43). For this one, his cross next to the cross of Christ was the ladder by which he stole into heaven. The other thief struggled against the cross. He did not turn to the suffering Christ, but in his own suffering added to the sorrows of Christ Crucified by blaspheming and reviling his Saviour.

These three crosses represent the three classes of men Christ invites to follow after Him in the carrying of His cross. The cross of Christ represents the innocent. The cross of the Good Thief represents the repentant and shows forth the plentiful redemption of Christ on the cross. The cross of the other thief represents the impenitent and unrepentant. Here on Calvary, suffering as Christ suffered, this last group of men will even then reject the grace and mercy of God. The innocent and the repentant follow after Christ with good will, with patience, with submission, and with joy. They realize that the cross of Christ is their salvation. The impenitent reject this grace. They come indeed to the crossroad, but they take the wrong turn and their cross becomes for them an instrument of damnation.

Look on Jesus Christ, the cross-bearer. See Him who sustains the world itself, all bruised and broken and bleeding – sustaining the weight of the cross. Jesus falls under the cross. It nearly overwhelms Him, yet He would not part with it for all the comfort in the world. He will not give up the cross, for it is His glory. However, He will share it. He will let all men suffer with Him. By the wood of the cross He will free these from their sins.

Look upon Christ as He bears His cross. Did any have crosses as heavy as His? Did ever things look so black and dismal as they looked to Christ on His journey? Yet He kept carrying the cross. It is the royal road to victory over sin, the devil, and death.

True Christians should patiently carry the cross with Christ, and never forget that all sorrow is a share in His cross. Remember that He is always present to help. Bear the cross for Christ. In this way, you will find your whole life is easier and happier and the reward of heaven will be yours:

"For if any man will come after me," cries our blessed Lord, "Let him deny himself, take up his cross daily, and follow me" (Lk. 9:23).

"And I, if I be lifted up, will draw all things to myself" (Jn. 12:32).

How to Meditate Further on This Chapter

COMPOSITION OF PLACE

a) *Physical:* The Way of the Cross. The brightness of noonday in an oriental city. The deadly heat. The dust of the city street milled up by the crowd of onlookers. The dead weight of the cross. The many falls of Jesus. His apparent weakness. The burning desire of His enemies that He must live to be crucified. The unwillingness of anyone to help Him. The compelling of a stranger to take the cross up after Him.

b) *Spiritual:* Once again there is no one willing to go the whole way with Jesus. His heart has been both moved and comforted by the appearance of His Mother. The charity of Veronica has made the malice of the rest stand forth more ignominiously. The tears of the holy women have been balm to His soul. But still no man will come forth to help Him. None will accept His invitation to take up the cross and follow Him. And His only helper must be forced onto His side.

WHO IS IT THAT SUFFERS?

This is the Good Jesus. Our Redeemer. Our Saviour. Our model and exemplar. He could have had heavenly hosts carry His cross. But He does it alone. He is God who has made men from the dust of the earth. He now falls into this dust again and again. In these last hours He gives marvelous example of the power of the cross. Of its merit and its virtue. And tremendous mercy. He is willing to share it with a man. With us.

WHAT DOES HE SUFFER?

a) *Spiritually:* He suffers that His cross is so despised. He suffers that His efforts to save men are so misunderstood. He suffers that there is no one willing to help Him. He suffers from the blindness of the Chosen People who will not recognize Him. He suffers from the indifference of the soldiers too proud to help Him. He suffers from the multitude who have so quickly forgotten His healing ministry to them. He suffers that none of His own come forth. He suffers that Simon must be forced into service.

b) *Physically:* Jesus Christ is suffering in every part of His body from the scourging. His holy head is crowned with thorns. He suffers from the great weight of the cross beam of His instrument of death. The holy St. Gertrude in pious conversation with her mystical Spouse heard Him complain of the unremembered wound in His shoulder which caused Him excruciating pain. He is overcome with weakness for it is almost eighteen hours that He has gone without food or drink. Each fall weakens Him more. In truth can He cry out in the Good Friday liturgy . . . "My people, my people! What have I done to thee or in what have I offended thee . . . for thou hast prepared for Me . . . the cross."

c) *Mentally:* Jesus suffers because so few are willing to accept the opportunity of bearing and sharing His cross with Him. He suffers in His loneliness. In being despised. In being unaided. In being friendless. In the inability of those who love Him most to assist Him. And in the outright refusal of those who could help Him to do so. He suffers because so many others in the centuries to come will refuse the cross and will not carry it. In the numbers to come, who like Simon will have to be forced to carry the cross against their will.

WHY DOES HE SUFFER?

a) *Chronologically:* In time Jesus suffers as the scapegoat of old, which was laden down with the sins of the people and driven out into the wilderness to be devoured by wild beasts. He carries not only the weight of the wood of the cross, but the intolerable weight of all the sins of our sinful race. He carries the cross to prove His love. He bears the cross to set us an example. He walks the way of Calvary like a Lamb that is led to the slaughter. Jesus Christ is our Cross-bearer. He walks the weary way in our place and for our sins. He walks this way to give each of us an opportunity to follow after Him.

b) *Mystically:* Jesus carries His cross, and shares it with a man to invite us to follow after Him and take up our cross. He carries His cross because we are afraid to carry ours. To teach us that without the cross there is no part with Him. That His burden is light and His yoke is sweet. That we must carry our cross according to the testimony of the Good Thief . . . "justly because of our sins."

WHAT AM I GOING TO DO ABOUT IT?

Resolutions: I will accept as coming from the hands of God whatever cross He may send me. I will accept the cross in atonement for my sins. I will take up my cross so that I may follow after Jesus and walk in His footsteps. Since He has been willing to suffer so much for me, I will be willing to accept every suffering out of love for Him. I will never forget that even my worst pains will only be splinters from the cross. I will be resigned to God's will and offer it up for my sins.

PRAYER

Almighty and everlasting God, who in order to give an example of humility to the human race, didst cause our Saviour to take up our flesh and to carry the cross, mercifully grant that we who have seen this testimonial of His patience may merit to share in the promise of His resurrection. Through the same Christ our Lord. Amen.

ASPIRATION

"We adore Thee, O Christ, and we bless Thee, because by Thy holy cross Thou hast redeemed the world" (*3 years' indul.; Racc. No. 191*).

The Hour of Triumph

THE Crucifixion is the focal point of all history. In the history of man, it is the longed-for act of redemption and restoration to grace. In the personal history of Jesus Christ, it is the day and the hour for which He was born and for which He came into the world. In the history of the Sacred Passion itself, the Crucifixion is the climax of the love of Jesus and of the hatred of His enemies.

Because of the tremendous significance of the Crucifixion, the medieval appreciation sent minds and men into a frenzy of effort to portray its deepest meaning. Great importance was attached to even the least details.

It was fitting, they taught, that Christ should be sacrificed at high noon, because the official Jewish sacrifices were in the morning and in the evening, and since Christ's sacrifice was to excel both, it was fitting the two should be brought together in time at noon. The teaching of St. Thomas on the becomingness of Jerusalem as the place for Christ's death was well received. His reasons were that it was the place chosen by God for sacrifice;

that the crowds there for the feast would make His death more humiliating, and the spread of the knowledge of it would be rapid.

A pious pilgrim, by the name of Ralph, startled Christendom with the observation that Christ died in Jerusalem because it was the geographical center of the world. This, he insisted, could be proved scientifically by the fact that when at high noon he stuck his pilgrim's staff in the ground it cast no shadow. The gullible rejoiced at this new mystical discovery. Soon the theory was blasted when a few enterprising monks found that in many places a stick would cast no shadow at high noon.

Regardless of what we might advance and believe as the reasons for the time and place of the death of Jesus, the Gospel makes it clear that it was the hour and place of His own choosing. "No man taketh my life away from me, but I lay it down of myself. And I have power to lay it down; and I have the power to take it up again" (Jn. 10:18). "Wherefore Jesus also, that he might sanctify the people by his own blood, suffered without the gate" (Hebr. 13:12).

When the doleful procession of the way of the cross reached Calvary, the last scene of the Passion was unfolded. "And when they had come to the place which is called Calvary, they gave him wine to drink mingled with myrrh, and when he had tasted he would not drink. And it was the third hour and they crucified him" (Mk. 15:22).

Here we see that the usual procedure in crucifixion was followed. The Victim had already been scourged, so He was offered a drug to reduce Him to a state of stupor on the cross. But Jesus, after tasting the bitter potion in order to increase His sufferings, would not consume the rest, as He wanted to suffer in the full possession of His senses.

There were two methods of crucifixion. In the first, the upright beam of the cross was permanent. The victim was nailed to the crossbar on the ground; then the victim and crossbeam were hoisted by ropes and fixed in place. Finally the feet were nailed to the cross. The second method, which Christian art seems to prefer, was the nailing of the victim to the full cross on the ground and setting it in place. Leaving to the experts the problem of which method was used, let us consider the torments Jesus Christ endured when nailed alive to the cross. The shock of spiking hands and feet to the rough wood of the cross sent strong men writhing in pain so that several assistants were needed to keep the victim in place. Jesus, however, is the victor even in this hour, and submits with greatest restraint of natural impulses and infinite resignation to the violent pain. The first shock of being lifted up on the cross, with the dead weight of his body pulling every joint and socket, was enough in some cases to drive the crucified insane. Yet in this hour Jesus Christ thinks not of His own pain, but rather of its healing effects. "And I, if I be lifted up from the earth, will draw all things unto myself" (Jn. 12:32).

In accordance with the custom of the time, the clothes of the victim belonged to the executioners. "The soldiers therefore, when they had crucified him, took his garments (and they made four parts, to every soldier a part), and also his coat. Now his coat was without seam, woven from the top throughout. They said therefore to one another: Let us not cut, but let us cast lots for it, whose it shall be: that the scripture might be fulfilled, saying: They have parted my garments among them, and upon my vesture they have cast lots. And the soldiers indeed did these things" (Jn. 19:23, 24).

In order to ruin the reputation of Jesus in the sight of the people, two miscreants were crucified with Him, one on His right and the other on His left. These wretches had been scourged as a preliminary to their crucifixion. Both blasphemed God and Christ, feeling, no doubt, that the condemnation of Jesus had precipitated their own deaths. One of them cried out, "If thou be Christ save thyself and us" (Lk. 23:39). Then the grace of the Passion flowered into its first conversion, when the thief on the right raised the only voice on Calvary in defense of Jesus. "Neither dost thou fear God seeing thou art under the same condemnation? And we indeed justly; for we receive the due reward of our deeds, but this man hath done no evil" (Lk. 23:40).

And then the Good Thief made the classic understatement of all history. "He said to Jesus: Lord, remember me when thou shalt come into thy kingdom" (Lk. 23:42).

Jesus Christ is the Man of the Hour. Every hour is His triumph but never more satisfying than in His answer to the penitent thief. "Amen I say to thee, this day thou shalt be with me in Paradise" (Lk. 23:43).

The chief priests and ancients, gloating over the crucifixion, reviled Christ and invited Him to come down from the cross and they would be converted. Jesus saw their hypocrisy. If He had come down, they still would not have believed Him. If He had come down, He might have converted some five hundred souls on Calvary; then, for the rest of His life, people would say of Him, "There's the man who came down from the cross." So Jesus chose to stay. And now and forever He is adored and blessed because by His holy cross He has redeemed the world.

INRI

The Jewish leaders, who never seemed satisfied by anything about Jesus, now complained about the title over the cross. The title, or sign board, giving the reason for the death of Jesus, simply read, "Jesus of Nazareth, King of the Jews" (Jn. 19:19). Pilate had earlier insulted the proud leaders by calling Christ their king in sarcasm. In truth, he has written the title. The simpering chief priests solicited him, saying, "Write not the King of the Jews. But that he said: I am the king of the Jews" (Jn. 19:21). Pilate, seemingly fed up with their malevolence toward Jesus, although too late to help the Saviour, cut the whole business short by thundering, "What I have written, I have written" (Jn. 19:22).

We cannot think of the Crucifixion of Jesus without considering the great anguish and sorrow of His holy Mother. As St. Paul of the Cross so beautifully said, "Wherever the Son is, there is the Mother also." The medieval artists and devotees of Mary called her station at the foot of the cross the Transfixion of the Virgin, alluding to the prophecy of Simeon that a sword would transfix her heart. So carried away were they with compassion for Mary that they read their own reactions into her sufferings. Thus we find two typical medieval devotions condemned by the Church: The Swooning of the Virgin and The Spasm of the Virgin. In the light of the Gospel, the idea of Mary's collapse, or a fit of uncontrollable anguish, seems altogether out of place. For St. John describes Mary as a tower of dignified sorrow and fortitude, saying: "Now there stood by the cross of Jesus, Mary his Mother" (Jn. 19:25). Jesus gave the custody of His Mother to His beloved disciple, St. John. He gave the custody of the whole human race to her in turn.

It is precisely the sufferings of Mary at the foot of the

cross that have earned for her in time and in eternity the appellation, "Queen of Martyrs." It is the common teaching of the Fathers of the Church that the sorrow of Mary at the foot of the cross was so great that if God had not supported her, she would have died of grief. Thus, on the Feast of the Dolors of Mary, the Church makes bold to sing: "Blessed be the senses of the Blessed Virgin Mary, who without dying, merited the palm of martyrdom beneath the cross of the Lord." And St. Antoninus writes, "The martyrs offered their own lives; but Mary's martyrdom consisted rather in offering the life of her divine Son to God, a life incomparably dearer than her own." The pious practice was to represent martyrs with the instrument of their pain. It was fitting, then, that the medieval concept of Mary, Queen of Martyrs, should represent her with the dead Jesus in her arms, since compassion for His tortures was the cause of her martyrdom.

With a piercing physical and mystical thirst, an unparalleled desolation of soul, our Jesus after three hours of Crucifixion prepared to die of His own will. To the last moment of His last hour still the conqueror, Jesus with a loud voice made an announcement that shook the foundations of earth and hell and swung open the portals of heaven. "It is consummated. And bowing his head, he gave up the ghost" (Jn. 19:30).

Thus, with a dramatic touch, the Man of the Hour dies on the cross. From that hour to the present, the most noble treasure and most essential characteristic of the Church is the crucified Saviour on the wood of the cross. The enemies of the Church know this. When they wish to insult holy Church and mortify Christians, they take their revenge on the crucifix. The first step against the Church is always to tear down the crucifix. In their childlike fury and antipathy to the crucifix, they protest a great truth, that the one, holy, catholic, and apostolic Church was born from the lance-pierced heart of Jesus.

The lovers of Jesus also know the crucifix is the heart of Christianity. They wear it in life and bear it in death. St. Thomas tells us he obtained more wisdom from this book of the crucifix than from any other book. This book of love, this forbidden book among the enemies of God, can be read at a glance by all. The prophet attests to this: "I will take a book and give to him that knows not numbers and say: Take up and read" (Isa. 30:12).

In conclusion, every lover of the Crucified should be able to say with the dying St. Benitius, who called out for the crucifix, "Give me my book. Yes, this is my book, my dearest book. I have read it all my life long. With it I will bring my life to a close."

And so it is. In the beginning, now and forever, Jesus Christ is the Man of the Hour, and every hour is His triumph.

How to Meditate Further on This Chapter

COMPOSITION OF PLACE

a) *Physical:* The hill of Calvary. The place of the skull. The charnel house of the criminal dead. The nearby burial places. The darkened sun. The moon unwillingly apparent. The face of the earth clouded. The contour of the earth broken by quakes. The veil of the temple rent in two. The Holy of Holies laid bare to the shocked gaze of all. Jesus on His cross. Lifted up between heaven and earth. Between two thieves. The Magdalen and John. Mary keeping station. The soldier's lance. The dead Christ. The heart of God laid bare for men to see.

b) *Spiritual:* The climax of Christ's coming into the world. The baptism wherewith He was to be baptized. His long desired goal. His last proof of greater love than all men, as Jesus lay down His life for His friends. The end of the old law of hate and fear and retribution. The beginning of the new law of love and mercy and forgiveness. The end that is our beginning. The death that is life. The battle that appears a loss but which is in itself an everlasting victory over sin, death, and hell.

WHO IS IT THAT SUFFERS?

God Himself who gives to all men a sign. A sign of salvation. A sign of triumph. The life-giving sign of the cross. The Redeemer of the world who buys us back with the rare coin of His blood. The Saviour of the world who saves man from sin, from eternal death, from the unbridled sway of the powers of hell.

WHAT DOES HE SUFFER?

a) *Spiritually:* He suffers the indifference of men to His sufferings for them. From the ingratitude of sinners who dying in their sins will fling back all this suffering into the face of God. He suffers in the sufferings of those He loves. Of His mother. Of St. John. Of the Magdalen. In the disappointment of His disciples who did not recognize that the Christ had to suffer all these things and thus enter into His glory.

b) *Physically:* Here on the cross is the totality of Christ's outpouring of self for men. His copious redemption. Behold His head, crowned with thorns. Struck with reed sticks. Slapped with the mailed fist. Bedraggled and bespittled. His eyes closed in death. His lips parched and fevered. His tongue dried up like a potsherd. See His hands pierced with nails. Clenched by torment. Stained with blood. Consider His body. One great wound. From head to foot covered with cold sweat, warm blood, dirt and dust. Note His holy heart ripped by a lance and emptied of its natural fluids. Pause by His sacred feet. Gripped with the nail. Pinned to the cross. Awaiting your kiss.

c) *Mentally:* Before His death listen to your Saviour. He begs forgiveness for those who make Him suffer for they know not what they do. Hear Him cry out with the psalmist that He feels abandoned in the lower parts of His soul, despite the Beatific Vision that perdures always between Himself and His Father. See His grief over His mother. The indifference of those who make sport of Him. Who blaspheme Him. Who cast dice beneath His feet.

WHY DOES HE SUFFER?

a) *Chronologically:* He suffers out of love for men. He who so hates sin still loves the sinner. He who has been abandoned by men will not let them be forsaken. Here is the test of love. The greatest demonstration of God's love. That He should die for us. In our place. For our sins. That He should be the victim, and we the guilty should go free. That He should take the handwriting that was against us, and blot it out forever, by affixing it with Him to the cross. The only answer to such an outpouring of self is God's love for us. "He loved me, and He delivered Himself for me."

b) *Mystically:* If I were the only one who had ever sinned, so great is the love of God for me that He would still have come down from heaven and suffered and died, just for me. He died for me as an individual. My personal sins have nailed Him to the cross. And just as the foresight of my offences, negligences, and omissions caused Him this pain . . . so too, every sin I do not commit . . . every temptation I overcome . . . every evil I put to flight . . . is that much less for my Jesus to suffer for. Every act of penance and reparation I make is a consolation to Jesus in His Crucifixion in the mystical but nonetheless real Passion of Jesus.

WHAT AM I GOING TO DO ABOUT IT?

Resolutions: I will keep the image of Jesus Christ Crucified always before my eyes . . . at home and at work. I will always be grateful for what He has done for me. I will remember His Passion. I will thank Him. I will avoid sin. I will try to perform acts of mortification in honor of the Passion and death of Jesus, especially on Friday. I will make the Way of the Cross frequently to impress His sufferings on my mind and heart. I will compassionate the Sorrowful Mother of God and take my place with her beneath the cross. I will assist at Mass with the greatest devotion and never arrive late nor leave early, because the Mass is the representation of Calvary. I will frequently kiss the cross out of love for Him who died thereon. I will meditate a little every day on the Passion of Jesus asking myself with St. Paul of the Cross: Who is it that suffers? What does He suffer? Why does He suffer? And I will make holy resolutions and put them into practice by asking myself . . . What am I going to do about it?

PRAYER

"O God, who didst will to sanctify the standard of the life-giving cross by the precious blood of Thine only-begotten Son, grant, we beseech Thee, that they who rejoice in honoring the same holy cross, may rejoice also in Thine ever present protection. Through the same Christ our Lord. Amen. (*5 years' indul.; Racc. No. 212*).

ASPIRATION OF ST. PAUL OF THE CROSS

"O my Jesus, I thank Thee, for having died on the cross for my sins" (*300 days' indul.; Racc. No. 192*).